THE WORLD'S LIVING LANGUAGES

*Basic Facts of
Their Structure, Kinship,
Location and Number of Speakers*

SIEGFRIED H. MULLER

Chairman, Department of General Linguistics, Adephi University

*Former Director, Languages-of-the-World Archives
(U.S. Department of Education)*

FREDERICK UNGAR PUBLISHING CO.
NEW YORK

410
M 91 w

OMNIBUS LINGUAS AMANTIBUS

47,716
August, 1964

PREFACE

The widening range of nearly all peoples' activities has given rise not only to a realization of the need for better communication but also to an intensified intellectual curiosity regarding the extent, nature, similarity, and affinity of different languages and their cultural bonds. Linguistics, a relatively young science, tries to provide much of this information. As a pure science, linguistics poses a host of challenging problems for the researcher; as an applied science, it is bound to interest and aid anyone who deals with people speaking a foreign language or who is stirred by a sense of discovery when faced with an unfamiliar tongue.

This book has a twofold purpose. First, it aims to provide a survey of the languages presently spoken in the world, primarily from the descriptive linguistic, social, or anthropological point of view. Second, the book may serve as an up-to-date and statistically reliable reference work in which the languages are given in genetic, numerical, geographical, and alphabetic listings.

For 200 languages, this book records location and number of speakers, official status and self-designation, the relative importance, the phonemic, morphemic, grammatical, and lexical structure and kinship, written form where extant, and clues by which the idiom may be identified by sight and sound without a working knowledge.

The English names and spellings of the languages as given in this book were chosen after careful scrutiny of established usages in current professional and governmental publications with due consideration of descriptiveness and etymological soundness. Acceptable synonyms are listed in the general index as cross references to the adopted preferred form, but spellings that are clearly faulty or etymologically false are omitted in the hope that their fall into oblivion will be hastened.

The numbers of speakers given include only those to whom the language is native. There are, of course, many bilingual and multilingual persons who have a better knowledge of their acquired tongues than of their primary one; however, for lack of reliable data it would be impossible to classify a person under the language he handles best, and his inclusion among the speakers of his mother tongue results in more accurate statistics. The numbers of native speakers are based on the latest available data gleaned from a variety of sources with special emphasis on United Nations publications and official censuses. In many instances, evaluation of contradictory evidence necessitated drastic revision of previously accepted figures. Linguistic literature abounds with divergent numbers of speakers, often failing to take into account spectacular population changes. All larger figures are rounded off to the nearest million or five million depending on whether the language has under or over fifty million speakers.

In order to arrive at a meaningful comparison, calculations have been based on reasonable estimates of the status on January 1, 1964, when the world's population amounted to about 3,225 million. Considering that every minute there are over a hundred more people in the world, resulting in an average annual growth of 65 million—the equivalent of double the population of Spain or of the total of native speakers of French —care must be exercised in projecting figures for the future. For example, the most-spoken language, Chinese-Mandarin, gains 14 million speakers every year. Moreover, there must be taken into account not only the annual average growth of about 2 percent, but also the fact that this growth is far from uniform; it is as high as 2.8 percent in the world's less developed countries. Thus, the increase is greatest in Central America and the Middle East and smallest in northern and western Europe. Demographers have calculated that it will take only six years to add another half billion to the population of the world if the present trend continues; the languages favored for expansion are the Sinitic and Indic ones, as well as Arabic and Spanish.

The languages discussed in this book include 144 which have at least one million native speakers. Fifty-six languages with fewer speakers are mentioned for any of the following reasons: they were or are taught in the United States, constitute a known individual language family, provide a link in the establishment of kinship, or are of unusual political, cultural, anthropological, or linguistic importance. Although the book is predominantly synchronic (descriptive) in its approach, diachronic (historical) features are included where they are considered desirable to explain the present linguistic situation or are of special interest. This applies to several extinct languages, including seven that survive only in religious services.

All linguistic terms that occur in the text and are not explained there, are defined in a glossary.

TABLE OF CONTENTS

ix

TABLES

INTRODUCTION

A survey of languages should arrive at the number of languages spoken throughout the world. The figure of 2796, attributed to the French Academy,* has been repeated several times in linguistic publications. While this total may approximate the truth, it is foolhardy to cite such a precise figure. For one thing, we have little or no knowledge of over half of the world's languages; that these are spoken by less than 1 percent of the world's population, may make them less significant, but does not alter the fact that they exist. Whether they all constitute separate languages or are merely dialects is an open question. All languages undergo continuous changes in vocabulary, meaning, pronunciation, and grammar; these changes occur with varying degrees of intensity in different parts of the speech communities, so that dialectical divergences may in time yield new languages. Unfamiliar tongues are at present explored more eagerly than ever before, especially in Africa and the Western Hemisphere, but even if enough were known to identify and classify all idioms properly, one crucial question would remain, that is, whether we are dealing with a language or with a mere variant of one, a dialect.

This decision is in many cases a difficult and arbitrary one because an unequivocal definition of both terms is elusive and because there are many borderline cases. Generally speaking, variants become languages when they have developed to a stage

---

* First quoted in Louis H. Gray, *Foundations of Language* (New York, 1939), p. 418.

1

at which they are no longer mutually intelligible. Although this is true of several Italian dialects, we have, nevertheless, in the recognized standard Italian (a development of the Tuscan dialect) that every Italian learns in school, a common meeting-ground, so that the dialects are not considered separate languages. Another criterion is the degree of separate cultural development of groups of speakers. This justifies calling Dutch and Afrikaans separate languages even though they are mutually intelligible. Dutch and Flemish, on the other hand, are so similar that they should be regarded as the same language although they are spoken in different political entities. Obviously, many of these decisions are debatable. The educational background of speaker and listener enters into the question of mutual understanding, and prejudice easily interferes in forming opinions on a language's cultural independence.

Thus, a precise figure for the world's languages can never be established; in fact it would be of little value. The most accurate estimate is that there are about 2500 languages spoken in the world, exclusive of dialects, and that there is a possible correction of up to 200 above or below this figure. We also have some knowledge of about 250 extinct languages.

Languages may be classified according to various points of view. The geographical is a convenient approach, but scientifically the least satisfying, though it often coincides with linguistic similarities. On principles of structure, languages may be grouped into four broad categories: inflecting, isolating, agglutinative, and polysynthetic. Examples of these types are Russian, Chinese, Hungarian, and Basque respectively. A third method is the genetic, the one followed in this book. It seeks to establish kinship on the basis of comparison of common features and to trace the pedigree of related languages back to one ancestor, attested or deduced. In this way, a system of language families, which in turn may be subdivided into branches, groups, and subgroups, may be set up. As the precise number of languages is still unknown, the number of families is also uncertain. Moreover, the affinity of some languages and families has not yet been established beyond dispute. There are probably about one hundred families. The classification of this book subsumes the living languages under twenty headings, some of which are, for lack of information, geographical groupings representing an unknown number of families. The sequence of presenting the identifiable language families is based on the broad areas of their original habitats: Europe, Asia, Africa, Oceania, and America.

1. INDO - EUROPEAN LANGUAGES

Practically half the world's population, 1,580 million people, has as its mother tongue a language of the Indo-European family. Moreover, these languages are understood, read, or spoken by additional millions. All the idioms that have at various times held the status of world languages belong to this family.

The term *Indo-European* is derived from the fact that these languages were originally located in an area encompassed by Europe and India, but it should be borne in mind that not all the idioms now spoken within this territory are members of the same family and also that, by migration, Indo-European tongues have spread widely in all directions. They are now native to all continents and many islands, with one-fourth of their speakers outside the Eurasian area. Another term frequently employed for this family is *Indo-Germanic,* a name based on the fact that the easternmost language, Assamese, is an Indic tongue and the westernmost, Icelandic, a Germanic one.

1.1. Proto-Indo-European

It is believed that the Indo-European languages developed from one common idiom, *Proto-Indo-European,* spoken by one people possibly as early as 4000 B.C. As this antedates the invention of writing, we possess no records of it, but by pains-

taking comparison of the vocabulary and structure of the ob-
servable descendant tongues, a hypothetical mother language
has been deduced. It seems to have been endowed with a rich
inflectional system that was reduced in the daughter languages
to varying degrees.

The features, notably the word stock, of this reconstructed
language should reflect the people's way of life and reveal its
original habitat. Comparative linguistics provided valuable
clues on early Eurasian history to supplement the scanty find-
ings of archeology. Since all Indo-European daughter languages have words for *winter, cold,* and *snow,* and none for
tropical animals or plants, like *tiger, rice,* or *palm,* the prob-
able home was in the temperate zone; further ingenious studies
have revealed that the speakers may have lived in an area
where the birch and beech trees are native and where the
salmon spawned and bees existed. The region was thus narrowed to central Europe between the rivers Elbe and Vistula,
from where the people later fanned out in a southerly and
southeasterly direction. Other theories place them north or
south of the Black Sea.

At some time between 3500 and 2000 B.C., a division took
place into a western and an eastern branch, evidenced linguistically by the conversion of guttural sounds into stops in the
western division and into continuants in the eastern. An illustration of this process is the word for *hundred,* which became
centum, pronounced 'kentum,' in Latin and *satem* in Avestan.
The Western and Eastern branches are thus also referred to
as *Kentum* and *Satem* languages, now the native tongues of
some 830 and 750 million people respectively.

1.2. Germanic Group

In the course of its development, each of the two Indo-European branches split again into several linguistic groups. One
important division took place some time before 500 B.C. in

the western branch, resulting in the separation of a language now referred to as *Proto-Germanic,* also not attested. This cleavage is manifested by a systematic change of some consonants, called the Germanic Soundshift, which converted the voiceless tenues *p, t, k* into aspirates, the voiced aspirates *bh, dh, gh* into voiced stops, and the voiced mediae *b, d, g* into voiceless tenues. This phenomenon, established by comparison of the vocabulary of various Indo-European languages, was first formulated in 1822 by Jacob Grimm and is hence also called Grimm's Law. The causes of this soundshift are unknown, but the most plausible theories point to changes of climate or the influence of other languages.

From this new stage the Germanic languages, now native to 420 million people, evolved. They in turn may be divided into a small northern and a much more numerous and important western subgroup. An eastern subgroup, represented by *Gothic,* became extinct a millennium ago. The northern subgroup, spoken by 20 million people, includes *Swedish, Danish, Norwegian,* and *Icelandic;* the western subgroup of 400 million includes *English; German* with its offspring, *Yiddish* and *Luxemburgian; Dutch-Flemish* and *Afrikaans;* and *Frisian.*

ENGLISH

With 265 million, English has the second largest number of native speakers of the world's living languages. By migration, it has been carried over the entire world, farther than any other tongue, a fact which contributes to its importance today. Only one-fifth of all native English speakers, 56 million, are found in the British Isles, the language's base territory. In the Western Hemisphere it is native to about 165 million in the United States, 13 million in Canada, and over 3 million in former and present British possessions, including Jamaica, Trinidad, British Guiana, British Honduras, Barbados, the Bahamas, and other West Indies islands. A creolized variant is spoken by 80,000 in Surinam. In Africa, there are over 1 million speakers of English in the Republic of South Africa, about 1½ million each in Kenya and Tanganyika, about 1 million each in Ghana, Nigeria, and Uganda, and 3 million in a dozen additional regions. In Asia, there are 2 million in India to whom English is native, and 500,000 in Singapore, Malaya, the Philippines, and on the island of Borneo, with additional native speakers clustered in and around many port cities. Australia accounts for 11 million, New Zealand and Pacific islands for 3 million.

English is official in the United States and its dependencies, the United Kingdom, Australia, New Zealand, Liberia, and some thirty former and present English territories; it is co-official in Canada, Puerto Rico, Ethiopia, Cameroun, the Republic of South Africa, Ireland, and Pakistan. In India its co-official status is constitutionally guaranteed until 1965 and will most likely endure for some time although only 3 percent of the population can handle the language. In Kenya, where English is a minority language, it won a 1962 parliamentary decision over Swahili as the designated official tongue. It is one of the two "working" and five official languages of the United Nations.

As an acquired idiom, it is used by at least 200 million people. It is taught as a foreign language in the great majority of nations over the world; in the school systems of the non-English-speaking countries in the Western Hemisphere and in western, central, and northern Europe, it is the subject studied by most foreign-language students. The United States Information Agency beams English lessons by overseas television to an estimated audience of 25 million in thirty-five countries. The historical events of this century, the political importance of the United States, the influx of foreign students to institutions of higher learning in the United States and Great Britain, the educational aid rendered by these nations to less developed countries in Africa and Asia, the news media in the English language, all tend to increase the desire of foreign-language speakers to acquire a knowledge of English. It is the universal language of aviation, shipping, and sports. English has thus become the most international tongue of our time, and it may be estimated that up to 500 million people, or one-sixth of the world's population, have a working knowledge of it. About 70 percent of the world's mail is written in English, and 60 percent of the world's radio programs are broadcast in English.

The name *English* is derived from the language of the Angles, who came to Britain, with less numerous Saxons and Jutes, from their homes on the German and Danish shores, beginning in A.D. 449. These tribes settled in the eastern and southeastern parts of what later came to be known as England. Their Low German idioms in time replaced the indigenous Celtic tongue and amalgamated into what became known as *Anglo-Saxon,* now preferably called *Old English.* Danish rule in the ninth to eleventh centuries added other Germanic elements to the language, intermingling Scandinavian and Old English. The victory of William the Conqueror in the battle of Hastings in 1066 and rule by French kings until the thirteenth century brought an influx of Norman-French vocabulary, but the language remained essentially Germanic in its structure and basic vocabulary. However, many synonyms or near-synonyms entered into the word stock, which was subsequently further enriched by borrowings, principally from Latin, Greek, Dutch, Parisian French, other Romance tongues, and the idioms of the American Indians. By the sixteenth century, the English vocabulary contained words from fifty foreign languages. In recent years annual accretions and new coinages amounting to thousands of words far outweigh the number of words becoming obsolete, so that English has become the language with the richest vocabulary: modern dictionaries list around 600,000 entries. This compares with 50,000 in Samuel Johnson's first English dictionary of 1755.

During the period of *Middle English* (1150-1500), significant structural and morphemic changes took place. By 1500, inflections had been sharply reduced, and as the language became more analytic, word order was rigidified. Almost the sole remnants of the originally rich inflectional system are the third person singular present tense ending *s* in the conjugation and the plural *s* and so-called Saxon genitive endings in the noun declension: the sons, son's, sons'. In standard English, the guttural spirant fell into disuse, surviving only in the written form and in the Scottish dialect, from which we get the word *loch*. English and Icelandic are the only Germanic tongues that have retained the voiced and voiceless dental spirants but the English alphabet lacks symbols for them. The vowel values were affected radically.

Although the pronunciation of many words changed, their spelling was largely retained. As a result, English orthography no longer reflects pronunciation; its irrationality is a challenge to native and foreigner alike. The *sh* sound, for instance, may be spelled fourteen different ways, and the letter combination *ough* expresses eight different phonemes: "A tough, dough-faced ploughman [British spelling] went thoughtfully through the borough, coughing and hiccoughing." Conversely, the sentences "the sun's rays meet" and "the sons raise meat" have identical pronunciations. There have been several attempts to produce an alphabet with each of the forty basic sounds represented by a distinct symbol; so far, these have not been successful, nor has the movement toward "simplified spelling" achieved any appreciable results.

Speech divergences are greatest in England, where there are over twenty distinct dialects, and such extremes as the Cockney and Yorkshire dialects may be mutually unintelligible. The speech of aristocratic Londoners, known as the King's (or the Queen's) English, is looked upon as the standard for the educated. Differences between American speech areas are much less marked. The majority speaks General American, designated

as standard by the broadcasting companies. Its native territory is the Middle and Far West. Two other divisions are the Southern and the Eastern Standard, the latter spoken in New England and as far south as the Potomac River. Each has two or three subdivisions. The ratio of numbers of speakers is approximately 9:3:2. A special phenomenon is the "thoity-thoid street" speech of Brooklyn, which resulted from the substratal influence of the Dutch inhabitants of New Amsterdam on the speech of their English conquerors in 1664. Historically, American speech has not changed as much as British.

In spite of the large distances between the world centers of English speech, diversity has not been so intense as to result in distinct languages, and there is no lack of mutual intelligibility between speakers of the standard pronunciation of their respective countries. Differences are most noticeable between American and British English. In the spoken form they show in the intonation, the pronunciation of certain words (*bath, branch, clerk, derby, lieutenant, schedule*), or the accentuation (*advertisement, financier, laboratory*). In spelling, British English calls for *our* instead of *or* in words like *labour* and *colour,* and prefers *aluminium, connexion, defence, gaol, programme, storey* (floor), *advisor,* and analogous words. The greatest variation is semantic; not counting slang terms, there are about two hundred common words and expressions with radically different meanings in American and British English, especially in the realms of entertainment, household, clothing, communication, and transportation. The following may serve as an illustration: the British motor car (automobile) uses petrol (gas) and may be a saloon (sedan) with windscreen (windshield), demister (defroster), wings (fenders), buffers (bumpers), wireless (radio) with valves (tubes), sparking plugs (spark plugs), sump (crank case), gearbox (transmission), silencer (muffler), accumulator (battery), and dynamo (generator). The tools in the boot (trunk) include a spanner (wrench) and an electric torch (flashlight). The American hood is a bonnet,

whereas the British hood is the top. The car may be parked
in a car-park (parking lot), on the verge or heath (shoulder),
or on a lay-by (roadside park), but not on unadopted land
(private road), and it must not be driven on the pavement
(sidewalk) or grit (sand). A diversion (detour) from the dual
carriage-way (divided highway) to avoid a traffic block (jam)
or bends (sharp curves) may lead to a roundabout (traffic
circle), and one should watch for loose chippings (fallen rock).

In the eighteenth century, a trade jargon developed in South
China ports and gradually spread to the western Pacific islands.
Its designation, *Pidgin English,* is a garbling of *business English.*
It is simple English adapted to regional speech habits with a
vocabulary colored by the indigenous language of the district.
Thus, we have Chinese Pidgin, West African Pidgin, and the
like. To the latter belongs *Krio,* widely spoken as a second
language in Sierra Leone.

On and around New Guinea, Pidgin English has in a little
more than a hundred years evolved a form, *Neo-Melanesian,*
used as an indispensable lingua franca by 1 million people
who speak several hundred languages. It is based on about
six hundred English roots and a hundred native words, and
it forms additional needed terms by such circumlocutions as
cow oil for "butter," *grass belong head* for "hair," or *pants
belong letter* for "envelope." Grammar is greatly simplified or
almost lacking. The future tense of verbs is expressed by adding *bimeby* to the unalterable stem, the past by adding *finish.*
Pidgin English in New Guinea has newspapers, school books,
and foreign literature in translation, though the spelling is not
standardized.

In 1920, C. K. Ogden and I. A. Richards discovered that
complete communication is possible by the use of fewer than
one thousand English words. During the next ten years, Ogden
developed a quintessential language labeled Basic English,
consisting of 850 words, including only 18 verbs. The English

that resulted was correct, but condensed to the absolute minimum required for complete thought expression. It was proposed as a solution of the international language tangle because it would be as easy to acquire as some artificial tongues—an average time of sixty hours was found to be sufficient. Also, it had the advantage of being a natural language already spoken by a large number of people.

For two decades, Basic English enjoyed a considerable following of enthusiasts, backed by governmental leaders in the United States, the USSR, and Great Britain, but gradually the need arose for hundreds of additional specific words in science, economics, religion. The movement seems now to have become one more milestone in the search for the ideal means of international linguistic communication.

GERMAN

German (self-designation *deutsch*) is the official language of four countries in the heartland of Europe. The largest, Germany, is at present split into West Germany (Federal Republic of Germany), East Germany (German Democratic Republic), and the divided city of Berlin, with a combined total of almost 75 million speakers. To the south are Austria with 7 million, Switzerland with 4 million, and between them the small duchy of Liechtenstein, with only 17,000 speakers of German.

At many places, political and linguistic borders do not coincide. Languages overlapping into the area defined above include Danish, Frisian, and Slovenian; there is a small Lusatian enclave in East Germany, and in Switzerland, German is only one of four official languages, although it is the major one, spoken by 71 percent of all Swiss. Its Swiss territory is the northeastern part of the country, including the capital, Bern. Switzerland's other official languages are French, Italian, and Romansh.

German extends beyond frontiers into neighboring countries.

In France, Alsace is predominantly German-speaking. In the Italian province of Alto Adige, to which Austrians refer as Southern Tyrol, German is spoken by about 250,000 and has equal linguistic status with Italian, so that all public signs are bilingual. Although the region's capital, Bolzano, is easily recognized in the German name *Bozen,* some of the place designations vary widely, *Vipiteno* for *Sterzing,* for example. An estimated 3½ million speakers of German are located in Iron Curtain countries, especially in the Ukraine, Poland, Rumania, Hungary, and Yugoslavia.

Overseas, German speakers are located principally in the United States, in New York, Pennsylvania, the Middle West, and California. *Pennsylvania German,* often erroneously named *Pennsylvania Dutch* after its own word for the language and spoken by over 1 million people, stems from the speech of the German Rhenish Palatinate. The bulk of German migrants to America came from this region in the seventeenth century. German is numerically the largest foreign language spoken in the United States, being claimed in the 1960 census as a mother tongue by 4½ million persons. There are 500,000 speakers of German in Canada. Germans in Latin America total about 2 million and are most numerous in Argentina and Brazil, where some towns even have German names. The count of persons throughout the world for whom German is the mother tongue approaches 100 million. As an acquired language, it is used by additional millions, principally in southeastern Europe.

The linguistic affinity between German and English manifests itself in a certain correspondence between the phonemes of both languages. German lacks the dental spirants, however, and for four German sounds there are no equivalents in English. This comparison is admittedly an oversimplification as there are additional minor phonemic differences. German orthography is much more phonetic than English, and an acceptable pronunciation may be achieved by observing a few simple rules.

Vowels have cardinal values, are generally long in open syllables and short in closed ones. When doubled, they are always long. In *ie,* the *e* lengthens the *i;* similarly, *h* may serve to indicate a long preceding vowel. The umlaut *ä* has the same pronunciation as *e* in German and approximates English 'there.' The umlauts *ö* and *ü* have no equivalents in English; they correspond to the French *eu* and *u.* They are produced like German *e* and *i* but with the lips rounded. The three German diphthongs *au, ei* (also written *ai*), and *eu* (also written *äu*) approximate the sounds in English 'lounge,' 'lie,' and 'loin' respectively.

Among the consonants, it should be noted that *v* is pronounced like English *f,* and *w* like English *v.* German *z* is like *ts;* the *r* is uvular; final consonants are pronounced unvoiced even if spelled voiced; initial *s* is voiced; initial combinations *sp* and *st* are to be pronounced like *shp* and *sht* respectively. Two voiceless spirants do not exist in English and tend to give a guttural sound to German. One is a palatal fricative that somewhat resembles the sound following *c* in English 'cure,' but is much stronger; it is used after *l, n* and *r* and with front vowels. The other is a velar spirant, as heard in the Scottish *loch,* and is used after back vowels. In the first of these sounds, the front part of the tongue approaches the hard palate; in the second, the back part is raised toward the velum. Both sounds are written *ch.* They are referred to as the *ich* and the *ach* sounds, from these typical words meaning *I* and *oh.*

Much of the German word stock is similar to English, though some cognates may be deceptive, such as *Gift,* which in German means *poison.* Sentences like *Der Blinde hat einen goldenen Ring am Finger der Hand* or *Der Winter ist oft bitterkalt und der Sommer warm und mild* can be understood readily by a speaker of English. Nouns have three genders, and the choice of gender often defies rationalization. As to morphology, a rather full inflectional system exists for nouns, pronouns, and adjectives with a number of classes and as many as six different forms in each; on the other hand, the conjugation is comparatively simple. In spite of the verbal inflections, there is a rather rigid syntax, which differs from English in fourteen patterns. Characteristic are the inversion of subject and verb in the main clause if the subject does not begin the sentence, and the end position of the finite verb in dependent clauses.

The long compound nouns written as one word, or at best hyphenated, may reach staggering proportions; *Fernverkehrsbahnsteig* for "long distance train platform" and *Einkommensteuerveranlagungskommission* for "income tax assessment commission" are logical, though at first bewildering.

Dialectical variation within the German speech area is considerable and in extreme cases may reach the point where communication becomes a problem. The speech of 300,000 citizens of Luxemburg has diverged from standard German so much that it must be considered a distinct language, Luxemburgian (self-designation *lezebuurjesh*). In Germany, the main dividing line runs west-east approximately from north of Cologne to Frankfort on the Oder, separating the northern tongues, *Low German* (self-designation *plattdütsch*), from the *High German* (self-designation *hochdeutsch*) in the south. The terms Low and High relate to the elevation of the land, which gradually rises from the North Sea and the Baltic toward the Alps.

This linguistic difference may be defined as the High German Soundshift, also known as the Second Soundshift because it is a virtual repetition of the First, or Germanic, Soundshift that had affected all Germanic languages about a thousand years earlier. During the time of the migrations in the sixth and seventh centuries, a systematic change in the consonant system took place in the southern regions and was completed before the language was reduced to written form in the eighth century. Five consonants were affected to result in seven changes. The voiceless dental spirant, now written *th* in English, became the voiced dental stop *d;* the voiceless stops *p* and *t* became initially the affricates *pf* and *z* (pronounced *ts*), but *f* and *s* in final positions; the voiceless velar stop *k* became a spirant *ch;* and the voiced dental stop *d* became voiceless *t*. Knowledge of these regular changes makes it easy to deduce cognates in English. Examples are *dick, Pfund, Zinn, reif, Nuss, Storch,* and *Garten.* Low German words do not reflect the change and are often closer to English than to High German, as may be seen by comparing Low German *Piep, twe, wat, Bök, Door* to High German *Pfeife, zwei, was, Buch, Tür* and English *pipe, two, what, book, door.* As the dental spirant does not exist in German, the dental stop appears in both Low and High German: *Ding* "thing."

Historically, we differentiate *Old German* up to about 1050; *Middle German* to about 1500; and *New German* from then on. Literary and cultural achievements were always predominant in the south so that High German became the standard and is now the only form taught in all German schools and used on the stage and radio. The supremacy of High German was furthered by the compromise between north and south German speech striven for by Martin Luther when he translated the Bible in the beginning of the sixteenth century. The development of German classical literature in the eighteenth and nineteenth centuries as exemplified by Goethe and Schiller in Germany, Grillparzer in Austria, and Keller in Switzerland, all of whom wrote in a rather uniform High German, tended to fix this as the modern literary language and the standard in all German-speaking lands.

Nevertheless, present dialects within the High German area show considerable differences and may be broadly subdivided into *Middle German* in central Germany and *Upper German* in the south. To this latter group belong *Bavarian-Austrian* and *Swiss German* (self-designation *schwyzertütsch*), which is so different from standard High German that merchants frequently display signs to the effect that both German and Swiss German are spoken in their shops. Swiss German belongs to the Alemannic dialect, which gave the name to the French word for German, *allemand.* Characteristic of Upper German dialects are the lengthening and diphthongization of vowels, unvoicing of initial *s,* syncopation of the *e* in unstressed syl-

lables such as in the participial prefix *ge,* and omission of
final *n* in the infinitive. It seems reasonable to predict that
greater mobility of the people and the unifying effect of broad-
casts in the standard language will tend to reduce dialectical
variations.

Though Roman type, in German named *Antiqua,* is now in
general use, an older "German," or "Gothic," style, *Fraktur,*
with its own script is still employed in German printing to a
limited extent. This form of letters is similar to the English
black letter type, which, with its thick vertical strokes connected by slanting hair lines, was evolved by scribes in the
fourteenth century. The facts that printing was invented in
Germany about 1450 and that the first letters were cut in imitation of the then prevalent monastic style of writing may
explain why this type has survived. Its use has, however,
declined rapidly since World War II.

German printing fonts have thirteen lower-case ligatures. A
unique minuscule digraph, ß, expresses a sharp *s* sound. In
texts printed outside Germany, it is sometimes replaced by
ss or *sz* if the font lacks the proper character. Quotation marks
introducing a quotation are at the bottom of the line. Since
Danish abolished the capitalization of nouns, German is the
only language which writes all nouns with a capital letter. The
umlauts *ä, ö, ü* also help in the identification of written
German.

YIDDISH

Yiddish is spoken as a mother tongue by possibly 4 million
Jews, half of whom are now found in the New World, mostly in
and around New York City, where they constitute the largest
foreign-language group. In the USSR, the 1959 census men-
tions Yiddish as the native tongue of almost 500,000 people.
There, a half-hearted attempt was made in 1934 to foster
indigenous Yiddish culture by establishing the Jewish Autono-

mous Oblast in the Khabarovsk Kray around the city of Biro-
bidzhan. Other sizable Yiddish-speaking groups are found in
Israel, Argentina, Mexico, Rumania, Canada, and France.

The self-designation of the language is *yidish,* which means
"Jewish" in the language itself; but in speaking of the language in English, *Yiddish* and not *Jewish* should be used. In
New York City, there is a vigorous literature including drama
and journalism. The *Jewish Daily Forward* is the American
foreign-language newspaper with the largest circulation.

The tongue originated in the middle Rhine territory, from
which the Ashkenazic Jews were forced southward and eastward during the Crusades. They followed in the train of the
German colonizers, finally settling in a large territory from the
Baltic to the Black Sea. By the eighteenth century, Yiddish
had become the language of practically all Eastern European
Jews. Dialectically, there was a division into the southern u-dia-
lect in Poland and Rumania, used by three-fourths of Yiddish
speakers and the basis of the written form, and the northern
o-dialect extending into White Russia and Lithuania.

Yiddish is based on medieval German. While German under-
went substantial phonetic changes, Yiddish retained most of
its sound system so that it reflects better than modern German
the Middle High German of the thirteenth and fourteenth
centuries, especially in the vowels, the presence of the velar
spirant, and the lack of the palatal spirant. The basic word
stock is from the Middle German territory, with some Low
German and Upper German vocabulary interspersed. Up to
three thousand words were added from Rabbinical Hebrew,
and further admixtures came from Lithuanian, Byelorussian,
Polish, Rumanian, and Ukrainian, depending on the locality
of the speakers. In America, many English terms have been
absorbed.

Yiddish is written from right to left in Hebrew characters,
employing the vowel-points and some letters to represent vowel
sounds. It is the Germanic counterpart of Ladino in the
Romance group.

DUTCH - FLEMISH; AFRIKAANS; FRISIAN

The official language of the Netherlands, spoken there by almost 12 million, is Dutch (self-designation *nederlands*). A variant of it, Flemish (self-designation *vlaams*) extends southward into Belgium where it is the mother tongue of 5 million Belgians and has co-official status with French. Belgium is a bilingual country where the north, five-ninths of the population, speaks Flemish and the remainder French. The line of demarcation runs west-east with the capital, Brussels, barely north of it, although the city is predominantly French-speaking.

Both Dutch and Flemish represent separate cultural evolutions, best known in the realm of painting, but the linguistic variances, largely phonemic, are so minute that it is unjustifiable to speak of separate languages. The differences are much less than those between British and American English or between standard French and Provençal. The written form arose from the southern variant, Flemish, while the northern, Dutch, set the pattern for the spoken idiom.

Under the combining name of Dutch-Flemish, the language is native to over 17 million, which includes smaller groups in France, the Netherlands Antilles, and Surinam. In the United States, there are 140,000 foreign-born claiming Dutch as their native language and perhaps 100,000 second-generation Americans for whom Dutch is the mother tongue.

Afrikaans is the modern form of the language of the Boers, Dutch immigrants who established themselves permanently at Capetown in 1652 and later migrated northward. It may have arisen as a creolized language from an early Pidgin Dutch used in trade between colonizers and the natives. It is now the mother tongue of 2¼ million, or half the white population of the Republic of South Africa, and is co-official with English. Speakers of Afrikaans are mainly located in the northeastern section of the country, in Transvaal and the Orange Free State, but the language is also understood elsewhere; however, it is less used in Capetown Province and almost not at all in predominantly English-speaking Natal. Sizable groups of Afrikaans speakers are also in Bechuanaland, Basutoland, and Swaziland, so that the total number approaches 3 million.

In its written form it is only one hundred years old: the first Afrikaans book was published in 1861. It has completely displaced Dutch as the language of administration and education, and it may be expected that Afrikaans will continue to grow vigorously because its use is promoted as a matter of national pride and an expression of anti-British feeling. The future development of Afrikaans as a state-sponsored language undoubtedly parallels the progress of modern Hebrew.

The Frisian language (self-designation *friesisch*) is older than Dutch and probably the direct descendant of those idioms which resulted in the emergence of Old English. The total of present speakers is only 300,000. The largest concentration is in Friesland, the northernmost province of the Netherlands, where about 250,000 native speakers out of a population of 450,000 claim equal rights with their Dutch-speaking neighbors. About 5000 Frisians live on the German North Sea coast, another 12,000 on the German North Frisian Islands off Schleswig-Holstein, and about 30,000 in the United States.

These languages may be said to stand midway between English and German. They lean toward English in their morphology, toward German in their syntax and phonemes. Dutch has many characteristic diphthongs and triphthongs. Dental spirants are absent. It has a preference for the voiced velar continuant, as in the pronunciation of *g* and in the second part of the *sch* cluster, which in Afrikaans is pronounced and written as *sk*. Final consonants are voiceless but are spelled voiced. Dutch has a rather simplified inflectional system, though retaining three noun genders; in Afrikaans, inflection has dwindled to an almost complete loss of all endings except in the plural formation of nouns. Afrikaans has progressed farthest of all Indo-European languages on the way to becoming an isolating language. It has only one gender and strongly reduced word stems: *wa* "wagon," *het* "have," *oë* "eyes," from Dutch *wagen, hebben, ogen.* Dutch and Afrikaans word order is similar to German in the position of prefixes and verbs and in the inversion of subject and verb in main clauses if the first element is not the subject. Frisian manifests strong analogies with English.

Written Dutch and Afrikaans express long vowels by doubling; Frisian has the circumflex for the same purpose. Afrikaans and Frisian use the acute accent, but Dutch has no diacritics except the trema to indicate vowel separation. A vowel sound somewhat like that in English 'pain,' is rendered by *ij* in Dutch, but by *y* in Afrikaans. Quotation marks follow the German practice with the opening pair at the bottom of the line.

SCANDINAVIAN LANGUAGES

The four northern Germanic languages, Swedish, Danish, Norwegian, and Icelandic, derive from a common ancestor, *Old Norse,* which before the year A.D. 1000 was the only language spoken in Scandinavia and was referred to as *dönsk tunga,* "Danish tongue." Thereafter, migrations and historical events caused linguistic differentiation. Iceland was colonized around A.D. 870, chiefly by Norwegians. Other expeditions took Norwegians to Normandy and Greenland, and in the eleventh century, under Leif Ericson, to North America, while Swedish Vikings went eastward into Russia and the Balkans. If the inscription on the Kensington Stone (named after the place in Minnesota where it was found) is authentic, Swedes were in America as early as 1360. However, general opinion now considers this writing a hoax.

The nineteenth century witnessed considerable migration of Norwegians and Swedes to the American Middle West and to Canada, among other places. In some of the new territories, the Scandinavian tongue yielded to the local speech; in others, like Finland, it asserted itself. Nearly every port city on the Gulfs of Finland and Bothnia still has names in both Swedish and Finnish, as Helsingfors and Helsinki, Åbo and Turku, Kristinestad and Kristiinankaupunki.

More than any other Scandinavian tongue, Icelandic (self-designation *islenzka*), now spoken by about 130,000 of the 200,000 inhabitants of Iceland, has retained many of its original features. Owing to its geographical isolation, the influence of other languages has been negligible. Its literature, best known for the two Eddas, may go back as far as the tenth century. Icelandic has a full declensional system, while Norwegian, Swedish, and Danish have been reduced to a singular, possessive, and plural form. It has also kept three grammatical genders, whereas the other Scandinavian tongues have one common gender and a neuter form.

Written Icelandic still has separate letters for the voiced and voiceless dental spirants as in 'this' and 'thin' in the edh (ð) and thorn (þ). In modern inscriptions pretending to imitate Old English, the thorn is often mistakenly rendered by *y* as in "ye olde shoppe." The *a* and *o* umlauts are present in all Northern Germanic languages; in Icelandic writing they appear as the diagraph *æ* and *ö*. Of all Germanic languages, Icelandic alone uses the acute, which may occur over any vowel. The ending *-ur* on nouns and adjectives is unique. As in all other Scandinavian languages, the definite article is suffixed to the noun.

Faroese is an Icelandic dialect spoken by 30,000 on the Danish Faroe Islands where it is recognized as the official written medium of communication.

Swedish (self-designation *svensk*), with a total of almost 9 million speakers, accounts for half of the northern group. There are 7½ million in Sweden, where it is the official language with only Lapp as a linguistic minority, 1 million in the United States and Canada, and 500,000 in Finland and Estonia. There are two main groups of Swedish dialects, the Svea in the north and in Swedish-speaking parts of Finland and Estonia, and the

Göta in the south. The speech of Gotland is more archaic than the other dialects and deviates from them considerably. Swedish is co-official in Finland where it enjoys bilingual status rights in thirty-two communities. Forty-seven others have been declared monolingually Swedish, and there are four hundred thirty-eight Finnish-speaking communities.

Swedish has a strong musical pitch, and tonal patterns may carry semantic distinctions of otherwise identical words. Before a front vowel, *g* is pronounced *y*, *k* is pronounced *ch*, and *sk* is pronounced *sh*. The letter *å* is pronounced like *aw* in 'law'; the umlauts are written *ä* and *ö*, and these three letters follow *z* in the alphabetical order. Characteristic of Swedish orthography is the doubling of final consonants; the frequent words *ett*, "a," *att* or *till*, "to," and *upp*, "up," are recognition clues, as are also *jag* "I," *inte*, "not," and the most frequent Swedish word *och*, "and."

Norwegian (self-designation *norsk*) is spoken by a total of over 4 million, of whom over 3½ million live in Norway and 700,000 in the United States. This language is in the unique position of having two official forms; the two, *Bokmål*, "Book Language" (formerly called *Riksmål*, "State Language") and *Nynorsk*, "New Norwegian" (formerly called *Landsmål*, "Rural Language") are not so dissimilar as to exclude mutual intelligibility, yet the difference is striking. For example, Bokmål *Jeg har spist*, "I have eaten" in Nynorsk is *Eg har ete*.

Nynorsk, fashioned by Ivar Aasen in the 1850's out of country dialects, dominates the rural districts, especially in the west and central regions, while Bokmål is favored by 80 percent of the population, mainly in the cities and in southeast Norway. This is the language used by Ibsen. Laws may be debated and published in either language; both are used on the radio and for legal papers and forms; schools teach the idiom predominant in their particular districts, but have to acquaint all students with the other. There have been half-hearted attempts to create an amalgamated *Samnorsk*, "Common Norwegian."

The intonation also has a musical lilt, although it is generally less conspicuous than in Swedish. The *eg* combination is pronounced *ai*. The last letters of the alphabet are the digraph *æ*, indicating the *a* umlaut, the *φ* indicating the *o* umlaut, and the *å* pronounced as *aw* in 'law,' occasionally as *o* in 'low.' Exclusively Norwegian words are *å*, "to" and *opp*, "up."

Danish (self-designation *dansk*), spoken by almost 5 million in Denmark, is closest to Norwegian. Until 1814, Denmark and Norway were under one ruler, with Danish as the common official language. There are about 400,000 speakers of Danish in the United States. The musical pitch is lacking almost entirely. The alphabet is the same as in Norwegian. In 1948, the spelling *aa* was changed to *å* and the capitalization of nouns was abolished, which leaves German the only language capitalizing nouns. Exclusively Danish spellings are *af* "of," *at*, "to," and *op*, "up." Final consonants are never doubled in Danish. Like Norwegian, Danish uses a large number of letters that are not pronounced, and the stress is generally on the initial syllable.

ANCIENT WRITING

Old Norse used the oldest Germanic writing in the runes, "secret letters," which were in use in parts of Scandinavia as early as the third century and later yielded to the Roman letters of Christian missionaries. The twenty-four runic letters, later simplified to sixteen, are called *futhark* from the phonetic values of the first six symbols; they were probably adapted from Latin or Greek and may have been imported by early Norse traders who had dealings with the Greeks in the lands north of the Black Sea. The symbols' straight lines and sharp angles lent themselves to incision in stone, bone, or wood. There are some 2500 runic inscriptions, mostly in Sweden, all very brief, many of pagan magic content.

The written form of the now extinct Eastern Germanic language Gothic is preserved in an underground bombproof vault in care of the library of the University of Uppsala in Sweden. This priceless manuscript represents the earliest literature in any Germanic tongue. It is a fragment of the Gothic version of the greater part of the four Gospels of the Bible. This translation from the Greek was initiated by the Visigoth missionary bishop Ulfilas, who, for proselytizing purposes, invented the Gothic alphabet in the fourth century by adapting Greek letters. The Uppsala document was written in the fifth or sixth century on purple parchment; because of its predominantly silver characters it is named *Codex argenteus,* the "Silver Bible."

1.3. Romance Group

Languages of the Romance group are spoken by 390 million people as native tongues and by many more as acquired ones. Their common ancestor is *Latin.* They may be divided into an eastern group, closer to the parent Latin, and a western, which, by migration, extends far beyond its original home. The eastern group, spoken by 80 million, comprises *Italian, Sardinian, Rhaeto-Romanic,* and *Rumanian;* the western, with 310 million native speakers, includes *Spanish, Portuguese, Catalan, Ladino,* and *French,* as well as the creolized idioms *Papiamento, Portuguese Creole,* and *French Creole.*

LATIN

Closely bound to the history of Roman civilization is the life span of Latin, its development, spread, and influence on its descendant languages. The conquering Roman armies carried with them the colloquial idiom, Vulgar Latin, and it affected local vernaculars to varying degrees. At its greatest extent, about A.D. 117, the Roman empire encompassed all the lands on the Mediterranean Sea and in western and southern Europe, reaching from Britain to the Persian Gulf. Latin was the unifying speech of this multilingual realm. Thus it may be said that Latin, superseding Greek, became the second international language.

As the decline of Roman power in the fourth and fifth centuries caused withdrawal of Roman forces from the outlying provinces, the local vernaculars tended to relapse into their former state or become adapted to those of the new masters. In some lands, however, a form of Latin prevailed. A variation from the Roman standard was always noticeable, but with the rupture of communications, these dialectical differences became much more intensified. The result was the development of a number of tongues that, during the fifth to eighth centuries, became distinct idioms, the Romance languages. The conquest of Rome by peoples of Germanic speech portended the change of Latin to the form that later came to be known as Italian.

Latin was the universal tongue of all medieval universities; it experienced a revival in the fourteenth to sixteenth centuries when the Renaissance movement renewed interest in classical culture. Books were preferably written in Latin, and its use at Italian universities lasted into the nineteenth century. Legal documents and international communications were composed in Latin.

Progress in cultural and industrial activity requires constant additions to the vocabularies of all civilized languages, and next to Greek, Latin continues to be the largest reservoir of roots to be used for new terms. Such borrowings from Latin resort to the word stock of literary Latin, which deviated considerably from the vocabulary of the colloquial form, especially during the Golden Latin period, from Caesar to Augustus (81 B.C. to A.D. 14). The difference may be illustrated by borrowings from Latin in other languages; the literary term for "horse," *equus*, yielded *equine* and *equestrian*, whereas the colloquial term *caballus* is the basis for Italian *cavallo*, Spanish *caballo*, Portuguese *cavalo*, French *cheval*, and Rumanian *cal*.

Jerome's translation of the Scriptures into Vulgar Latin, the so-called Vulgate, in the latter part of the fourth century, fortified the establishment of Latin as the ecclesiastical language of the Roman Catholic Church, which still uses it for religious services and as a vehicle of international communication. Latin is an official language of the State of Vatican City, which publishes *Latinitas,* a quarterly written in Latin and dealing with contemporary secular topics. The expression of modern concepts in a revived Latin results in such renditions as *globus atomicus* for "atomic bomb" or *imaginum transmissio per electricas undas* for "television."

EASTERN SUBGROUP

Italian (self-designation *italiano*) is the native tongue of 55 million persons. 49 million live in Italy, 1 million each in France and Argentina, 500,000 in Brazil, and 300,000 in Yugoslavia. There are 3½ million speakers of Italian in the United States, where Italians constitute the second largest group among the foreign-born, and Italy ranks first in the listing of the countries of origin of first- and second-generation Americans. In Switzerland, Italian is one of four official languages and has 400,000 speakers in the canton of Ticino. The 20,000 inhabitants of the independent republic of San Marino also speak Italian.

Dialects vary tremendously, probably more than those of any other language. Several are mutually unintelligible; a Venetian is unable to communicate with a Sicilian if both use their dialects. Medieval Florence, in Tuscany, with its high regard for art and literature, was recognized early as a cultural center; here in 1582, an academy was founded for the purpose of purifying the Italian language. The first such establishment for any modern tongue, it was named *Accademia della Crusca* (*crusca* meaning "chaff"), and had a sieve for its emblem, symbolizing the intent to "winnow" the substandard from the approved literary forms. This movement naturally strengthened the recognition of Tuscan speech as the standard Italian.

The geographical location of Sardinia exposed its language to various Italian dialects from the continent, Corsica, and Sicily, as well as to Arabic and Spanish. As a result, Sardinian (self-designation *sardu*), constitutes a separate language, spoken by almost 1 million. It is split into five dialects, each reflecting the influences of the neighboring tongues. On the French island of Corsica, 300,000 speak Corsican, a dialect midway between Tuscan Italian and Sardinian.

Rhaeto-Romanic is a collective name applied to idioms spoken by close to 600,000 people and thought to be a survival of the Vulgar Latin used by Roman soldiers stationed in the southern Alpine valleys. The western form, Romansh, is native in the Swiss canton of Grisons and, though spoken by only 40,000, was recognized in 1938 as the fourth official language of Switzerland. Even this small group has dialectical variants, each with its own publications and each agitating for recognition as the standard. A central idiom, Ladin, is spoken by 20,000 in southern Tyrol, and an eastern dialect, Friulian, has 500,000 speakers in northeastern Italy near Austria and Yugoslavia. All Rhaeto-Romanic idioms show strong influences from the neighboring languages. Some confusion arises from the fact that the names *Romansh* and *Ladin* are often used interchangeably or even for all Rhaeto-Romanic dialects combined.

Spacially separated from the other eastern Romance languages is Rumanian (self-designation *româneşte*), which acknowledges its origin in its name. Of the 20 million speakers of Rumanian, about 17 million live in Rumania and 2½ million in the USSR. Most of these speak the Moldavian dialect and live in the Moldavian SSR, which borders on Rumania.

Syllables in the eastern subgroup of Romance languages are generally open. In Italian, all words end in a vowel, with the exception of some articles, prepositions, and disyllables which may drop the final vowel for the sake of euphony. The vowels have a full and invariable sound that makes the language admirably suited for singing. Rumanian has slight nasalization. Italian pronunciation makes a clear distinction between single and double consonants, the latter being given a more prolonged and emphatic sound. In Latin, the glottal spirant had become mute by the second century A.D. As a result, *h* is not pronounced in any Romance language, though it continues to be written. In Italian, *h* may serve to harden a preceding *c* or *g* when a front vowel follows.

As compared to the parent Latin, all descendant Romance tongues show a tendency to become analytic; Latin *feci,* "I have made," becomes Italian *ho fatto;* Latin *libri,* "of the book," becomes Italian *del libro.* However, the conjugation retains a rich inflectional system, and since the endings give precise information on person, number, tense, and mode, a pronoun subject is often omitted as unnecessary. Latin declension endings have all but disappeared; their function is taken over by articles and prepositions. Only in Rumanian is the definite article suffixed to the noun. Nouns are limited to two genders, masculine and feminine. The plural is formed by changing the final vowel, except in Rhaeto-Romanic which appends an *s,* following the western subgroup. With few exceptions, Italian possessive adjectives are preceded by the definite article.

The Romans learned the art of writing from the Greeks, through the Etruscans, and adapted the alphabet for their purposes. It has come down to us with minor changes, notably the addition of *j* and *w.* Roman letters have spread to many languages over the world and now serve more people than does any other form of writing. Within the past few decades, the Roman alphabet has replaced the use of Arabic in Turkish and Malay; it is being increasingly adopted by African languages, and Chinese and Japanese use it as an alternative to their native scripts.

Italian has no diacritics save an occasional grave over a final vowel either to indicate stress in a polysyllabic word or for semantic differentiation of homonyms. Spelling in Rhaeto-Romanic is far from uniform; some publications use no diacritics; others, the umlauts *ö* and *ü,* a grave, and a circumflex. Rumanian has the following characteristic letters: *ă* with a short *e* sound as in English 'quiet,' *î* with a sound similar to *u* in English 'cur,' *ş* and *ţ,* pronounced like *sh* and *ts* respectively. The Moldavian dialect of Rumanian is written with Cyrillic letters.

WESTERN SUBGROUP

The western subgroup consists of French and the Hispanic languages and their offspring. *Hispanic* is a collective name given to the idioms which arose on the Iberian Peninsula during seven centuries of Roman occupation and developed into their present forms after the withdrawal of Roman troops in A.D. 476. In consequence of migrations which reached large proportions after the discovery and conquest of America, four-fifths of all Hispanic speakers now live outside the Peninsula, mainly in Mexico, Central and South America, and the Antilles. On the shores of the Gulf of Biscay, *Basque* remains as the only non-Indo-European language and may be a remnant of the original indigenous speech of this area.

As a native tongue, Spanish (self-designation *español*) is spoken by 145 million persons. There are 35 million speakers of Spanish in Mexico, 23 million in Spain, 16 million in Argentina, 13 million in Colombia, 7 million each in Chile, Cuba, and Venezuela, 6 million in Peru, 4 million in Ecuador, 3 million each in the Dominican Republic and the United States, 2½ million each in El Salvador, Uruguay, and Puerto Rico, 2 million in Honduras, somewhat less in Bolivia, Guatemala, and Nicaragua, about 1 million each in Costa Rica, Panama, and Paraguay, and smaller groups in the Philippines, Morocco, and the Spanish possessions in the Atlantic Ocean and Africa.

The language is official in Spain and in eighteen Latin American republics. It ranks third as a mother tongue of United States foreign-born. It is administratively co-official with English in Puerto Rico and New Mexico. States with large Spanish-speaking populations include New York, Texas, Arizona, and California. It is one of the five United Nations languages. In Mexico and all countries of Central and South America, with the exception of Brazil and the Guianas, Spanish is the superimposed colonial language. In Paraguay, Spanish, although the only official language, is the native tongue of only slightly more than half the population; in Peru, Bolivia, and Guatemala, fewer than half of the inhabitants are native speakers of Spanish. Spanish is the most favored foreign language in United States school curricula. A creolized version, Papiamento, is spoken by 200,000 people of the indigenous stock in the Dutch West Indies islands of Curaçao and Aruba.

In Spain, there are a number of dialects; they do not vary to the extent of impairing intelligibility. The idiom of Castile, with Madrid as its center, is considered the standard, and the capital is also the seat of an academy intent on keeping the language pure. The educated Spaniard is likely to say that he speaks *castellano,* "Castilian," to stress the difference between it and other Spanish dialects or American speech.

One aspect in which Castilian and Latin American Spanish differ from each other is the pronunciation of *c* before *e* and *i* and of *z* before *a, o,* and *u.* In Castilian, these phonemes are dentals and sound like *th* in 'thin'; in America, they are alveolars and sound like *s* in 'sin.' More in Latin America and less in Spain, a final *s* is often slurred in careless speech. In Argentina, the so-called *yeismo* produces a pronunciation of *ll* and *y* similar to the *z* in 'azure.' Colombia is considered to have the best American Spanish pronunciation.

Deviations exist in the vocabulary, not only between Castilian and American Spanish, but also from country to country in the Western Hemisphere. Thus, a farm hand is *peón* in

Mexico, *guaso* or *roto* in Chile, *guajiro* in Cuba, Spanish *pata-tas,* "potatoes," are *papas* in America.

Portuguese (self-designation *português*) is spoken by a total of over 85 million which includes 72 million in Brazil, 9 million in Portugal, with its Atlantic islands, and over 3 million in African and Asian colonies. There are 200,000 Portuguese speakers in the United States. In addition, Galician, spoken by 2 million in Galicia, the northwestern province of Spain, is a Portuguese rather than a Spanish dialect. Portuguese Creole is the idiom of about 200,000 people on the Cape Verde Islands and in Portuguese Guinea.

Brazil is as large and populous as all other South American republics combined. The fact that its major and official language is Portuguese is the result of Pope Alexander VI's division of the world into Spanish and Portuguese spheres of influence. In 1493, he drew a line of demarcation from the North Pole southward; it cut through the eastern tip of South America, conferring on Spain a monopoly west, and on Portugal, east of this line. The following year, the line was moved westward to longitude 50° west of Greenwich, thus awarding to Portugal control over the bulk of the coastal areas of what became Brazil. Subsequent Portuguese explorations east of this line led to the establishment of colonies in Africa and Asia, notably Angola, Mozambique, Timor, and Macao, whose combined population exceeds that of the mother country.

Differences between the speech of Portugal and of Brazil exist in grammar, vocabulary, and pronunciation, but they are not very great. Brazilian Portuguese is more archaic and conservative, but at the same time has been influenced by Indian languages. It does not broaden the final *s* to *sh*. There are two main varieties, the Carioca of Rio de Janeiro and the Paulista of São Paulo, Brazil's largest city. Since 1943, a joint language committee has attempted to standardize Brazilian Portuguese and bring it closer to the language of Portugal.

Catalan is spoken by about 5 million in Catalonia, with Barcelona as its capital, on the Balearic Islands, and in a small

region in southern France. It has no official status in Spain,
but it is the only and official language of the tiny landlocked
republic of Andorra, the population of which is 10,000.

Ladino, the Romance counterpart of the Germanic Yiddish,
is the mother tongue of about 140,000 Sephardic Jews. They
live mostly in Turkey, Greece, and Bulgaria, especially in
Istanbul, Izmir, Salonica, and other eastern Mediterranean
ports, where their ancestors settled after their expulsion from
Spain. By recent migration, 20,000 live in Israel. Ladino is
basically fifteenth-century Spanish with admixtures from Hebrew, Greek, and Turkish. It retains many archaic words and
forms that were current in medieval Spanish. A comparatively
rich literature dates back to the sixteenth century.

French (self-designation *français*) is the native language of
almost 65 million. In Europe, 44 million speakers of French
live in France, 4 million in southern Belgium, 1⅓ million
in five western cantons of Switzerland, 300,000 in Italy, 100,000
in the British Channel Islands, 20,000 each in Monaco and
Luxemburg. In Africa, there are 1 million French speakers
in Algeria and 5 million in former French and Belgian possessions, in French Somaliland, on Réunion and the Comoro
Islands. In the Western Hemisphere, there are 5 million in
Canada, 1⅓ million in the United States, mainly in the
north by migration from Canada and in Louisiana, and over
500,000 in Haiti, Martinique, Guadeloupe, and French Guiana. Another 500,000 are to be found in the rest of the world,
including European countries, the Levant, southeastern Asia,
and Pacific islands.

Aside from territories and dependencies, French is official in
twenty-one independent countries, France, Monaco, Haiti, and
eighteen African nations, that emerged from former colonial
status: Burundi, Cameroun, Central African Republic, Chad,
the two Congos, Dahomey, Gabon, Guinea, Ivory Coast, Malagasy, Mali, Mauritania, Niger, Rwanda, Senegal, Togo, and
Upper Volta. In addition, the language is co-official in seven
nations: Algeria; Belgium, where it is known as Walloon;

Cambodia; Canada, where it is the mother tongue of 28 percent of the population; Laos; Luxemburg; and Switzerland,
where French speakers constitute 22 percent of the population;
and on the British island of Jersey.

French is probably second only to English as an acquired
tongue. Next to English, it is the most-studied foreign language
in the school systems of western Europe. During the seventeenth to nineteenth centuries, French had the status of an
international language previously held by Greek and Latin.
All diplomatic relations between nations of different speech
were preferably conducted in French, especially in the Balkans
and the Middle East. The international esteem of French is
evident in its use by the Universal Postal Union. French is one
of the five official languages of the United Nations and shares
with English the designation of "working language." Some of
the new countries in Africa have their native anthems in both
French and the indigenous tongue.

The language at the time of Charlemagne bore a strong resemblance to Latin; that form is now referred to as *Old French*.
It is first attested in a document which records the Strasbourg
Oaths of 842, juxtaposing the same text in *romana lingua,*
"Old French," and *teudisca lingua,* "Old German." Since that
time, several idioms developed on the soil of France, but the
political concentration in the capital, Paris, helped to make
Parisian French the standard for the country. In Paris, too, in
1694, the first dictionary was completed by the French Academy, a body founded by Cardinal Richelieu in 1635 to act as
supreme arbiter of the language.

Several dialects still prevail but they present little communication difficulty. One main cleavage is between northern and
southern speech, broadly labeled *langue d'oui* and *langue d'oc*.
These terms illustrate the development of the northern and
southern French word for "yes" from the Latin phrase *hoc illud
est,* "that is so." In the north, the three vowels of the first two
words were scrambled to yield *oui;* in the south, only the first
word was used, with the usual suppression of the *h* sound. The

southern idiom, Provençal, was in full glory in the twelfth century when it developed an impressive literature; during the Crusades, it became the first lingua franca, an expression which literally means "French language." Provençal is now spoken by several million people in a number of variant forms.

An odd development of the French language took place in Haiti, where it is official and employed in all publications and in higher learning. There the standard French is used only by the educated classes, less than 10 percent of the population. The idiom of the common people has deviated so greatly, because of considerable admixtures from African tongues, that it cannot be considered a mere dialectical variation and has become a distinct language with the name of French Creole (self-designation *français-créole*), spoken by 4 million. The two idioms are not mutually intelligible. Efforts are now being made to create a written standard and to teach French Creole in schools. Forms of French Creole are also found in Louisiana, Guadeloupe, Martinique, and French Guiana. The French speech of the natives of Réunion and the British island of Mauritius in the Indian Ocean has experienced a somewhat similar development. French Creole is the mother tongue of a total of 5 million persons.

In all Romance idioms, the *d* and *t* are true dentals and not alveolars. Characteristic of Hispanic languages are the palatalized *l* and *n,* as heard in English 'million' and 'canyon.' Spanish has a bilabial spirant, written *b* or *v,* and the voiceless velar spirant as in Scottish *loch,* written *g* or *j.* Diphthongization of Latin monophthongs is observed in Spanish: Latin *ferrum,* "iron," becomes Spanish *hierro,* and Latin *bonus,* "good," becomes Spanish *bueno.* The inability to begin a word with *s* followed by a consonant leads to prosthesis of *e,* as in *escuela,* "school," *español,* "Spanish," or *estación,* "station," even to the omission of the *s* in careless speech. In Portuguese, except in Brazil, a final or preconsonantal *s* is pronounced *sh.* Portuguese and French have nasal sounds. French has four, illustrated by the phrase *un bon vin blanc,* "a good white wine."

More than in any other Romance language, French phonemes deviate from the Latin heritage, possibly because of the Celtic substratum. Its uvular *r,* its vowels, and *o* and *u* umlauts resemble the German. French spelling is very unphonetic, using many silent letters. A final *e* is usually not sounded except for special effects in singing. Likewise, final consonants are mostly mute unless followed by a word which begins with a vowel and has a close syntactical relationship to the preceding one. In that case, a linking, *liaison,* takes place; for example, *nous,* "we," is sounded as *noo,* but the combination *nous avons,* "we have," is pronounced *noozavong.* The large number of silent syllables makes French one of the fastest-spoken languages with an average of three hundred fifty syllables per minute.

The grammar of the western subgroup generally shares the features of the eastern group. Nouns have two genders and lack endings except for the plural, which appends *s* with agreement in the adjectives, whether used attributively or in the predicate. The conjugation has a wealth of inflections. In the Hispanic languages, but not in French, a pronoun subject is usually omitted as redundant. In Spanish, a duplicating pronoun is generally used in addition to an indirect personal object. A special feature of French is the partitive article which is required where none is used in other languages, as in *du sel et de la viande,* "salt and meat." The absence of noun inflections causes strict adherence to word order rules. Object pronouns have to precede the verb in a definite sequence.

Though the Hispanic languages are closer to each other than to Italian or French, they are not mutually understandable without study. While Portuguese may at times appear deceivingly similar to Spanish, a comparison of even ordinary words will reveal striking differences, as may be seen by Spanish *ventana, comer, hablar, gracias,* and Portuguese *janela, jantar, falar, obrigado,* meaning "window," "eat," "speak," and "thank you." These languages, notably French and Spanish, have made large contributions to the English vocabulary.

With the exception of Ladino, which uses a modified Hebrew alphabet, all languages of the western subgroup use Roman letters, but each with distinctive combinations or diacritics. The palatalized *l* and *n* phonemes occur in Spanish as *ll* and *ñ*, as *lh* and *nh* in Portuguese, and *ll* and *ny* in Catalan. Both are considered individual letters and follow *l* and *n* in the alphabet. The Spanish *tilde* (˜) as used in the *ñ* is found in Portuguese, here called *til*, over an *a* or *o* to indicate nasalization. A final *m* in a monosyllable in Portuguese also nasalizes the preceding vowel and is itself not pronounced in that case. In Spanish, after *g*, a *u* before *e* or *i* is silent and serves to make the *g* hard; if the *u* has a diaeresis, it is pronounced somewhat like English *w*. Portuguese, French, and Catalan use the cedilla under *c* to indicate a sibilant before *a, o,* or *u.* French has a special digraph *œ* which occurs before *u;* the *o* umlaut is indicated by it or by *eu,* whereas the letter *u* is always sounded as the *u* umlaut.

Spanish is the only language that uses an inverted question mark (¿) or exclamation mark (¡) before a question or exclamation. The only accent occurring in Spanish is the acute, which may serve to differentiate homonyms as *de* "of," and *dé* "give," or to indicate a word stress that does not follow the rules: a word ending in a vowel or *n* or *s* is stressed on the penultimate, other words on the last syllable. The same holds true for Portuguese, except that *m* takes the place of *n* and a final *ã* is usually stressed. Portuguese uses the acute and circumflex for phonemic distinction and at the same time for the stress. The grave is used only to indicate an open sound value of *a, e,* or *o* regardless of the stress.

French also uses the three accents. The acute can stand only over *e,* the grave only over *a, e,* and *u,* the circumflex over any vowel. Accents are used in French for the indication of pronunciation of the vowel or for the semantic distinction of homonyms, but never for word stress, which is usually on the last pronounced syllable. The acute and circumflex often replace an *s* that has dropped out at some time in the history

of the French language, as in French *été*, "summer," derived
from the Latin *aestas*. The English speaker will easily find
cognates of *éponge, étable, état, forêt*.

1.4. Celtic Group

Before the Christian era, idioms belonging to the Celtic
group were spoken in most of central and southern Europe and
extended east as far as Asia Minor. One of the more important
languages was *Gaulish,* which yielded to Latin and had some
influence on the later evolution of French. Surviving Celtic
tongues are spoken by 3 million people who occupy various
areas in the British Isles and in northwestern France. These
languages are subdivided into a northern subgroup, *Goidelic,*
and a southern subgroup, *Brythonic*.

Included in the Goidelic subgroup are *Gaelic* proper (self-
designation *gaeilge*), spoken as a native tongue by 900,000 in
the western and northern counties of Ireland and 50,000 in
Great Britain's Northern Ireland, and *Scottish Gaelic* (self-
designation *gaelig*), with about 100,000 speakers in the northwest Scottish Highlands. A small group of speakers of Scottish
Gaelic is located in Canada, on and around Prince Edward
Island.

Gaelic is attested since the fifth century; beginning in the
eleventh century, it had one of the richest literatures of medieval Europe. In 1927, when Ireland was established as a sover-
eign state, Gaelic was declared co-official with British and its
use made compulsory in all schools, but most inhabitants continue to speak English. Although the revived interest in Gaelic,
furthered by national pride, has not been as successful as was
hoped, it may be assumed that the number of native speakers
will increase in future generations.

From the fifth century on, Gaelic was brought by Irish emi-
grants to Scotland where it developed its own literature and
was the language of the Court until the eleventh century. It

has been waning in recent times. A dialect of Scottish Gaelic, Manx, originated on the Isle of Man, but has lost ground during the last two hundred years so that it is practically extinct, being spoken by perhaps a few hundred people. Nevertheless, the island is not bound by the laws of the British Parliament unless they are promulgated in Manx, so that at an annual ceremony laws are publicized in both English and Manx.

To the Brythonic subgroup belong *Welsh* and *Breton*. Welsh is spoken in Wales and, by migration, in the United States, principally in Pennsylvania mining districts, by a total of about 1 million; Breton is the mother tongue of 1 million in Brittany.

Next to English, Welsh (self-designation *cymraeg*) is the most widely spoken language in Britain, and it is growing in popularity. The British Broadcasting Company has regular programs in the Welsh language, and primary schools in larger communities in Wales conduct classes in Welsh. Literature begins in the sixth century; most celebrated is the Mabinogion, a thirteenth-century collection of Welsh tales with themes belonging to the Arthurian legend. The yearly Eisteddfod is a congress of bards and men of letters who gather to keep Welsh poetry alive. Welsh is the mother tongue of over 700,000, about one-fourth of the population in Wales, but most speakers become bilingual, and only 50,000 continue to speak Welsh exclusively.

Typical of Welsh spelling are the *dd* and *ll* combinations, with a pronunciation similar to the English voiced *th* and voiceless *thl* respectively.

Breton (self-designation *breiz*) is not a descendant of ancient Gaulish, but was brought to the northwestern section of France, called Brittany, formerly Armorica, by immigrants in the fifth and sixth centuries. It comprises four distinct dialects, but most Bretons speak French also, and no Breton dialect is taught in schools. A distinctive letter is *ñ*, indicating a nasalized *n*. Diacritical marks used are the acute, grave, and circumflex over the *e*.

Characteristic of Celtic languages is lenition, the phonetic change of initial consonants determined by the final sound of the preceding word; a knowledge of the rules of mutation is necessary to find a word in the dictionary. Thus, Gaelic *dourn,* "hand," becomes *ho tourn,* "your hand"; Welsh *pen,* "head," becomes *fy mhen,* "my head," and *ei ben,* "his head"; Breton *kalon,* "heart," becomes *ar galon,* "the heart," and *me halon,* "my heart."

The Goidelic languages have retained a moderate inflectional system with four cases in the noun declension. Their spelling is somewhat archaic with the pronunciation deviating from it considerably. The Brythonic languages have simplified the declension to one case, and their orthography is more phonetic.

In the fifth and sixth centuries, Old Gaelic used so-called *ogham* writing, chiefly on tombstones. It was a system related to the Norse runes and consisted of twenty letters shaped as points and lines appended to a center line. The modern Gaelic alphabet of eighteen characters was derived in the eighth century from semiuncial Latin writing. It uses an acute to indicate a long vowel and a dot over consonants to denote aspiration. The other Celtic languages are written with Roman letters.

1.5. Greek

The great contributions of Greek culture to western civilization are well known. The evolution of the Greek language manifests a number of noteworthy facts which, considered singly or in combination, show that this language occupies a somewhat unique position. First, like Albanian and Armenian, Greek has not become diversified; second, although older than most Indo-European tongues, Greek has changed comparatively little; third, it was the first idiom to achieve the status of a world language, having served in the Mediterranean Basin as

lingua franca, named *koiné,* "common," before and during the
Roman empire, evidenced by the fact that the New Testament
was written in Greek; fourth, more than any other tongue, it
has contributed loan words to all other European languages;
fifth, it is in Greek that we have the oldest writing of any
European and possibly any Indo-European language.

Native speakers of Greek (self-designation *ellinika)* number
close to 10 million, of whom 8 million are located in Greece
and on its islands in the Ionian and Aegean seas. There are
500,000 in Turkish coastal towns and 450,000 in Cyprus, where
they constitute four-fifths of the population. In the United
States, there are 400,000 native Greeks. Smaller Greek communities are found in other countries, especially those bordering
on the Mediterranean and Black seas. Greek is the official language not only of Greece and Cyprus, but also of the autonomous gynophobic monks' republic of Mount Athos.

Phonemic characteristics are the voiced and voiceless dental
spirants as in English 'this' and 'thin' and the palatal and
velar spirants as in German *ich* and *ach.* The grammar has an
extremely rich inflectional system in declension of nouns, adjectives, pronouns, and articles, and in conjugation. Verbs have
a complete passive voice system and verbal aspects. One aspect
applies to a continuing action; the other, usually called
aorist, shows an action completed or occurring only once.

It was established in 1953 by Michael Ventris that the so-
called Linear B script on Minoan clay tablets is in Greek.
These were found on Crete in the first decade of this century
and date from the fifteenth century B.C. Thus they are the
oldest Greek writings, proving that Greeks knew how to write
half a millennium before Homer. These tablets show pictographic and syllabic characters. The Linear A writing, which
goes back another two centuries, is claimed by Cyrus H. Gor-
don to be *Phoenician,* establishing a cultural tie between Greek
and Semitic cultures. For the way of writing which later developed into the Greek alphabet and came down to us through
the Romans, the Greeks are indebted to the Phoenicians, whose

writing system they adopted in the ninth century B.C. By using
some symbols for the values of vowels, not indicated in Semitic
writings, and by adding other symbols of their own, the Greeks
created a sequence of twenty-four letters, named *alphabet* from
the names of the first two letters, alpha and beta, the names
themselves being Greek adaptations of their Semitic counterparts. At first, the direction of writing followed the Phoenician, running from right to left: later, a system called *bou-
strophedon* had alternate lines in reverse; this finally led to
the practice of writing consistently from left to right.

Later developments include the creation of minuscules and
diacritical marks including the three accents, acute, grave, and
circumflex, the latter appearing as ˜ or ˆ , to indicate vowel
length, and two breathing marks on initial vowels, the *spiritus
asper* (˘) to denote the presence, and the *spiritus lenis* (ʾ) the
absence of aspiration. In Roman transcription, the former is
usually rendered as *h,* and the *spiritus lenis* is disregarded. In
modern Greek, all vowels are of equal length and there is no
longer any initial aspiration, but the breathing marks are still
written, as are the accents, which have become mere stress
marks. With the exception of ten frequent monosyllabic words,
every word must have an accent. Accents and breathings are
placed over the second letter of a diphthong and in front of
capital monophthongs. A subscript iota under alpha, eta,
omega, introduced around A.D. 1200, is still written, although
it has no effect on the pronunciation. Punctuation marks include a raised dot (·) to indicate a colon or semicolon, and the
semicolon (;) is used as a question mark. The biologist's symbols for male and female (♂, ♀) originated from the Greek letters
theta and phi. These were the initial letters of the words
thouros and *phosphoros,* names given by the Greeks to the
planets Mars and Venus, respectively.

Changes that took place around 1100 in the transition from
Ancient to *Modern Greek* are mainly phonemic; a trend developed toward analytic structure, but the changes are relatively minor so that a native Greek has less difficulty reading

TABLE I
THE GREEK ALPHABET

Letter		Name	Modern		Ancient Where Different	
			Trsl.[1]	Approx. Equival.	Trsl.[1]	Approx. Equival.
A	α	alpha	a	lark		
B	β	beta[2]	v	vine	b	bad
Γ	γ	gamma	y[3]	yes	g	gold
Δ	δ	delta[2]	dh	this	d	din
E	ε	epsilon	e	lend		
Z	ζ	zeta[2]	z	zeal		
H	η	eta[2]	i	marine	e	vein
Θ	θ	theta[2]	th	thin		
I	ι	iota	i	marine		
K	κ	kappa	k[4]	kind		
Λ	λ	lambda[2]	l	lane		
M	μ	mu	m[5]	mad		
N	ν	nu	n[6]	name		
Ξ	ξ	xi	x	tax		
O	o	omicron	o	lock		
Π	π	pi	p[7]	pad		
P	ρ	rho	r	rain		
Σ	σ,ς[8]	sigma	s	seal		
T	τ	tau[2]	t[9]	tip		
Y	υ	upsilon	i[10]	marine	y	French tu
Φ	φ	phi	f	fine		
X	χ	chi	kh	loch		
Ψ	ψ	psi	ps	lips		
Ω	ω	omega	o	lone		

NOTE:

[1] Scholars do not agree on a standard key for transliterating Greek into English. The system here presented is a compromise and avoids diacritical marks.

[2] Beta, delta, zeta, eta, theta, lambda, tau are the names still in common use in English; in Greece, they are now called vita, thelta, zita, ita, thita, lamvtha, taf.

[3] Transliterate "n" before gamma, kappa, xi, or chi; "gh" before a back vowel or liquid; mute initially before kappa.

[4] Transliterate "g" after gamma.

Homer in the original than a speaker of English would have reading Old English. Conversely, a scholar of classical Greek is able to handle modern Greek if he allows for the phonetic changes. In the vowel system, there is no longer any difference in length between *o* and *ω* or *ε* and *αι*; six vowels and diphthongs *η, ι, υ, ει, οι, υι* have coalesced to yield the sound of *i* as in 'marine.' As an example of this radical vocalic change, the words *οἱ υἱοί*, "the sons," have changed in pronunciation from *hoi hyioi* to *iyi*. The upsilon as the second letter of a diphthong has become a consonant. The main consonantal change is the development of fricatives: the pronunciation of *β, δ, γ* changed from *b, d, g* to *v, dh, y*. In the case of *γ*, this change is limited to its position before a front vowel; before other vowels it has the sound of *gh* as in German *ich*. However, later developments and especially the need for transliteration from other languages, required the rendition of the *b, d, g* sounds by the somewhat clumsy combinations of *μπ, ντ, γκ* respectively, as exemplified by Μπώφαλλο, Buffalo, or Λένινγκραντ, Leningrad.

The Greek language has served admirably in supplying a large amount of vocabulary to all western languages, especially for scientific terms. In many everyday words, the Greek origin is no longer felt as foreign in the language. English dictionaries usually list Greek roots and affixes, and these continue to be resorted to for new expressions. The twelve percent of Greek works in the English vocabulary may not seem excessive, but numerous words are included which would be difficult to paraphrase by indigenous terms. All these loan creations were and are made with the classical phonetic values so that we get *biology* instead of *viology,* for instance.

---

[5] Mute initially before pi.

[6] Mute initially before tau.

[7] Transliterate "b" after mu.

[8] Second minuscule for final position in a word.

[9] Transliterate "d" after nu.

[10] Transliterate "v" after alpha or epsilon, "u" after omicron.

Modern Greek struggles with a linguistic cleavage that had its beginnings centuries ago, between the *katharevousa,* the so-called "pure tongue," and the *romaic* or *dhimotiki,* the "people's tongue." The divergences are less in pronunciation, more in grammar, and considerable in vocabulary: the words for "beer," "wine," and "bread" are *zythos, oinos,* and *artos* in the *katharevousa,* but *birra, krasi,* and *psomi* in the *dhimotiki.* At the time of the restoration of Greek independence in 1832, the *katharevousa* became designated as standard written language. It has the backing of government officials, clergymen, and scientists; it is used in parliament, by all newspapers, and in school books. It adheres to tradition, its orthography seeking to perpetuate the practice of over two millennia, but it is not used in conversation. The *dhimotiki,* on the other hand, reflects the modern development of the language. It evolved a literary form in the eighteenth century. Since 1917, it has been permitted in the lower school grades. Every Greek speaks it, but it has no dictionaries. It uses simplified grammatical forms and many loan words, mainly from Turkish, Albanian, and Italian. A process of amalgamation of the two forms has been striven for, but a uniform language is far from being achieved.

1.6. Balto-Slavic Group

Languages belonging to the Balto-Slavic group are native to 270 million people, a population extending from central Europe through the Asiatic USSR to the Pacific Ocean. The Baltic subgroup has about 5 million speakers and the Slavic subgroup is native to over 260 million people.

The Baltic tongues show such marked differences from the Slavic that they are sometimes treated as a separate group altogether. One of the living Baltic tongues, *Lithuanian* (self-designation *lietuviškai*), is spoken by 3 million people, of whom over 2½ million live in the Lithuanian SSR and the remainder in various colonies abroad, including 300,000 in the

United States. Lithuanian has preserved archaic features that make it especially interesting to the historical linguist; they seem to be survivals of Proto-Indo-European. *Latvian* (self-designation *latviski*) is spoken by over 1 million people in the Latvian SSR.

The Slavic subgroup may be divided into an eastern section spoken by 180 million people, located within the USSR, a western one spoken by 50 million, mainly in Poland and Czechoslovakia, and a southern one by 25 million, chiefly in Yugoslavia and Bulgaria. All the Slavic languages are thought to be descendants of a hypothetical *Proto-Slavic,* which is believed to have been the uniform speech of all Slavs around the time of Christ.

The principal languages of the Slavic eastern section are *Russian* with a total of about 135 million, *Ukrainian* with 38 million, and *Byelorussian* with 7 million speakers. Approximately 112 million speakers of Russian (self-designation *russki*) live in the Russian SFSR, 8 million in the Ukrainian SSR, another 13 million in other Soviet republics, and the remainder in other countries, including 1½ million in the United States. There are 33 million speakers of Ukrainian (self-designation *ukraïnski*) in the Ukrainian SSR, where they constitute three-fourths of the population, 4 million in other Soviet republics, and over 1 million in other countries, mostly the United States and Canada. Speakers of Byelorussian (self-designation *bielorusski*) exceed 7 million, of whom 6 million live in the Byelorussian SSR (White Russia) and 1 million in other Soviet republics.

The 1959 census of the USSR lists one hundred eight different ethnic origins for its population, and their idioms belong to at least six different families. Slavic tongues constitute only a little over three-fourths of all the languages spoken in the Soviet Union. Russian is the mother tongue of 83 percent of the population of the Russian SFSR, and it is also heavily represented in the other fourteen Soviet republics; in one, the Kazakh SSR, it actually surpasses the indigenous Kazakh. The

Moscow dialect is the basis of the literary tongue. Russian is one of the five official languages of the United Nations, and in the curricula of the schools of the Iron Curtain countries, the study of Russian is promoted vigorously as a matter of political expediency.

The western block of Slavic languages adjoins the eastern and extends into central Europe. Most important is *Polish* (self-designation *polski*) with a total of 33 million speakers, including 29 million within Poland, 3 million in the United States, where it holds fifth place in the numerical order of the mother tongues of the population, and close to 1 million in the USSR and other countries.

The two official languages of Czechoslovakia are *Czech* (self-designation *česky*), spoken there by 9 million and in the United States by almost 1 million, and *Slovak* (self-designation *slovensky*), spoken by 4 million. They are rather similar, diverging less in morphemes than in phonemes, as is apparent from the alphabets, in which some letters have different diacritics. The two languages are practically always mutually intelligible, which has led some linguists to consider them dialects of one language, to be designated *Czechoslovakian,* but the existence of varying letters and of individual literatures speaks against such fusion.

The least widely spoken Slavic language, *Lusatian* (self-designation *serbski*), is still the mother tongue of over 100,000 people who have been surrounded by German speech territory for centuries. This enclave is situated in East Germany, south of Berlin. Here the river Spree branches into over two hundred arms forming islands that in earlier times could be easily defended against marauding neighbors. Although the territory is relatively small, two distinct dialects developed, the Upper Lusatian, centered in the city of Bautzen and showing influences of Czech, and the Lower Lusatian, which is closer to Polish and has the city of Cottbus as its center; most speakers of Lusatian live in the rural districts.

Spatially separated from the other Slavic languages are those belonging to the southern block, whose linguistic confines more or less coincide with the national boundaries of Yugoslavia and Bulgaria. Yugoslavia is a federation of six republics with three official languages. The principal one is *Serbo-Croatian*, spoken by 8 million people in the republic of Serbia, which includes the national capital, Belgrade, by 4 million in Croatia, and by 3 million in Bosnia and Herzegovina and Montenegro. There are also about 300,000 speakers of Serbo-Croatian in the United States. Serbo-Croatian is the combining name of one language, referred to by the Serbs, who write it with Cyrillic letters, as Serbian (self-designation *srp),* and by the Croats, who write it with Roman letters, as Croatian (self-designation *hrvat).* Some newspapers print identical editions in both scripts. Serbo-Croatian is distinguished among Slavic languages by its musical intonation and clear vowel sounds. *Slovenian* and *Macedonian* are the two other official languages of Yugoslavia. Slovenian (self-designation *slovenski),* with fewer than 2 million speakers, is the language of the republic of Slovenia in northwestern Yugoslavia and of a small adjoining territory in Italy and Austrian Carinthia. Macedonian (self-designation *makedonski)* is spoken by over 1 million in the republic of Macedonia, situated in the southeastern corner of Yugoslavia, and overlaps into western Bulgaria and northern Greece.

Bulgarian (self-designation *bulgarski)* has 7 million speakers in Bulgaria and adjoining countries, especially the USSR and Hungary. The Bulgars are not of Slavic origin, but they conquered Slavic tribes and adopted their language. *Old Bulgarian* is the name sometimes given to *Old Church Slavic* which is preserved in documents dating back to the tenth century and is still used as a liturgical language by the Orthodox Slavs.

The Slavic languages have in general lagged in following the same direction of development as most western European languages and have retained a greater variety of inflections. Verbs have durative and perfective aspects to denote a continuous or completed action; some verbal endings differ according to the gender of the subject. Nouns, adjectives, and pronouns have three genders and a rather full declension, usually with seven cases: nominative, vocative, genitive, dative, accusative, locative, and instrumental. An exception is Bulgarian, which discarded case endings and became analytic, using prepositions to express grammatical relationship. The high degree of inflection permits free word order in the sentence. In Bulgarian and Macedonian, the definite article is suffixed and an indefinite article exists as a separate word; all other Balto-Slavic languages lack articles.

In the matter of vocabulary, the basic words show considerable resemblance, much more so than in the Germanic or Romance groups. Phonetically characteristic are a high degree of palatalization, a profusion of sibilants and gutturals, and a clustering of consonants. Words, especially prepositions, may consist of a single consonant that is sounded in combination with the following word. The *l* and *r* may become vocalic phonemes so that seemingly unpronounceable words like Czech *prst,* "finger," and *vlk,* "wolf," or Croatian *vrt,* "garden," are heard as *perst, velk,* and *vert.* Polish is the only Slavic language that has nasals. To express these phonemes in writing, the alphabets either have distinct letters or create variations of existing ones by superscripts, subscripts, and other diacritics.

The western Slavic peoples, who came under the influence of the Roman Catholic Church, employ the Roman alphabet, with changes characteristic of each language. The eastern nations, affiliated with Eastern Orthodox Churches, use a form of writing based on the Cyrillic alphabet, so named after its reputed inventor Cyril, a Macedonian missionary monk who together with his older brother Methodius set out to Christianize the Slavs in the ninth century. Paralleling in a way the work of Ulfilas, which in the fourth century led to the creation of the Gothic alphabet, Cyril based his writing on an imitation of Greek characters in order to translate the Gospels from Greek into Slavic. Characters were also adapted from other writing systems or were freely invented to render Slavic phonemes that the Greek language did not possess. Palatalization or the lack of it, for instance, may be indicated by a subsequent *myakhky znak* (Ь), the "soft" sign, or *tverdy znak* (Ъ), the "hard" sign, respectively.

While Cyrillic writing was at first completely phonetic, later changes in the languages created and widened a gap between the spoken and written forms so that the present script is, in most Slavic languages, no longer an exact reflection of the pronunciation. In several Slavic tongues there have been orthographic reforms, beginning with those of Peter the Great for Russian in the eighteenth century.

Table II shows forty-four Cyrillic characters in current use; certain ones are selected for each of the six main languages that employ this alphabet—Russian, Ukrainian, Byelorussian, Serbian, Bulgarian, and Macedonian. A scrutiny of this table reveals that some characters can be used initially in some languages and not in others and that some have varying sound values in different Slavic tongues or do not agree with the sounds of their Greek and Roman counterparts. The Ukrainian *eh* (#42) is virtually a different letter in that it faces the opposite way in Russian and Byelorussian. A knowledge of the symbols and their application is an aid in the identification of the individual languages.

The relative wealth of forms makes it possible to adapt the Cyrillic alphabet to other languages. In the Soviet Union an endeavor has been under way to extend the use of Cyrillic to several languages of other families, notably Caucasian and Uralic-Altaic, that formerly used different writing systems. The Cyrillic alphabet has also been seriously considered as a substitute for the Chinese writing.

The phonetic differentiation which Cyrillic provides by the inclusion or omission of certain letters is achieved in the languages using the Roman letters primarily by diacritical marks. Accents in use include the acute, circumflex, and the inverted circumflex; they always indicate a phonemic change, never word stress.

In Polish, the nasals are indicated by a hook under the

vowel: *ą, ę*. Other characteristically Polish letters are *ó, l* with a
bar (*ł*), standing generally for a sound similar to *w* in 'west';
ć, ń, ś, ź, and the *z* with a superscript dot *(ż)*, to indicate palatalization. Polish and Lusatian are the only Slavic languages
using the *w*, pronounced *v*. The *z* in Polish often serves to
palatalize a preceding consonant, and the combinations *cz,
dz, dź, dż, rz, sz, szcz* are frequent.

Czech obtains the same result with an inverted circumflex,
introduced by Jan Hus in the fifteenth century, so that the
Czech letters and combinations, *š, č, šč* correspond to the
Polish *sz, cz, szcz*, the phonemes for which Cyrillic has the
letters Ш, Ч, Щ. The inverted circumflex over *š, č, ž* appears
in all languages except Polish. Where this mark cannot be
placed on top of a tall letter, it may be affixed to the side:
Czech *dˇ, tˇ, Slovak lˇ*. Sometimes, this adscript is shortened
to an apostrophe: *d', t', l'*. The acute over a vowel indicates
lengthening; the *u* may have a circle over it: *ů*. Thus, Czech
has the following characteristic letters: *á, dˇ, é, ě, i, ň, ř, tˇ,
ú, ů, ý*. Slovak has the same letters as Czech, but lacks the
ě, ř, ů and adds *ä, lˇ, ô*, and *ŕ*. The *r* with an acute or inverted circumflex or followed by *z* is palatalized and forms
in the western Slavic tongues a peculiar phoneme, a close
fusion of *r* and *zh* or *sh*. The Czech composer Dvořak is pronounced *Dvorzhak*. Croatian may have the acute only over *ć;*
it also has the distinctive letter *đ*. Lusatian has *ě, ł, ř*, and the
acute over *b́, ḿ, ń, ó, ṕ, ẃ, ź* to indicate palatalization. Table
III shows how typical Slavic phonemes are expressed in the
different languages.

Lithuanian indicates former nasalization by a hook under
ą, ę, į, ų. It shares with the Slavic tongues and with Latvian
the symbols *š, č*, and *ž*. In addition, Lithuanian has *ł, ū, ů*,
and *ż*. Latvian uses the macron to indicate long vowels: *ā,
ē, ī, ū;* typical letters are also *ġ, ķ, ļ, ņ, ŗ*.

ALPHABETS OF CYRILLIC ORIGIN

TABLE II

#	Letter	NAME[2]	EASTERN SLAVIC			SOUTHERN SLAVIC			Trsl.[3]
			Russian	Ukrainian	Byelorussian	Serbian	Bulgarian	Macedonian	
1	А а	ah	А а	А а	А а	А а	А а	А а	a
2	Б б	beh	Б б	Б б	Б б	Б б	Б б	Б б	b
3	В в	veh	В в	В в	В в	В в	В в	В в	v
4	Г г	geh	Г г	Ґ[4] ґ[4]	Г[4] ґ[4]	Г г	Г г	Г г	g[4]
5	Ѓ ѓ	gyeh	–	–	Ґ ґ	–	–	Ѓ ѓ	gy
6	Д д	deh	Д д	Д д	Д д	Д д	Д д	Д д	d
7	Ђ ђ	dyeh	–	–	–	Ђ ђ	–	–	dy
8	Е е	yeh	Е е	Е[5] е[5]	Е е	Е е	Е е	Е е	ye[5]
9	(Ё) ё	yo	(Ё) ё	–	(Ё) ё	–	–	–	yo
10	Ж ж	zhe	Ж ж	Ж ж	Ж ж	Ж ж	Ж ж	Ж ж	zh
11	З з	zeh	З з	З з	З з	З з	З з	З з	z
12	И и	ee	И и	И[9] и[8]	–	И и	И и	И и	i[9]
13	Й й	ee kratkayah	(Й) й	Й й	(Й) й	–	Й й	–	y
14	І і	ee	–	І і	І і	–	–	–	i
15	Ї ї	yee	–	Ї ї	–	–	–	–	yi
16	Ј ј	yota	–	–	–	Ј ј	–	Ј ј	j
17	К к	kah	К к	К к	К к	К к	К к	К к	k

TABLE II

ALPHABETS OF CYRILLIC ORIGIN

#	Letter	NAME [2]	EASTERN SLAVIC			SOUTHERN SLAVIC			Trsl. [3]
			Russian	Ukrainian	Byelorussian	Serbian	Bulgarian	Macedonian	
18	Ќ ќ	kyeh	–	–	–	–	–	Ќ ќ	ky
19	Л л	el	Л л	Л л	Л л	Л	Л л	Л л	l
20	Љ љ	lyeh	–	–	–	Љ љ	–	Љ љ	ly
21	М м	em	М м	М м	М м	М м	М м	М м	m
22	Н н	en	Н н	Н н	Н н	Н н	Н н	Н н	n
23	Њ њ	nyeh	–	–	–	Њ њ	–	Њ њ	ny
24	О о	oh	О о	О о	О о	О о	О о	О о	o
25	П п	peh	П п	П п	П п	П п	П п	П п	p
26	Р р	err	Р р	Р р	Р р	Р р	Р р	Р р	r
27	С с	es	С с	С с	С с	С с	С с	С с	s
28	Т т	teh	Т т	Т т	Т т	Т т	Т т	Т т	t
29	Ћ ћ	tyeh	–	–	–	Ћ ћ	–	–	ty
30	У у	oo	У у	У у	У у	У у	У у	У у	u
31	(Ў) ў	oo	–	–	(Ў) ў	–	–	–	w
32	Ф ф	ef	Ф ф	Ф ф	Ф ф	Ф ф	Ф ф	Ф ф	f
33	Х х	khah	Х х	Х х	Х х	Х х	Х х	Х х	kh
34	Ц ц	tseh	Ц ц	Ц ц	Ц ц	Ц ц	Ц ц	Ц ц	ts

#	Letter	NAME[2]	EASTERN SLAVIC			SOUTHERN SLAVIC			Trsl.[3]
			Russian	Ukrainian	Byelorussian	Serbian	Bulgarian	Macedonian	
35	Ч ч	cheh	Ч ч	Ч ч	Ч ч	Ч ч	– –	Ч ч	ch
36	Џ џ	dzheh	–	–	–	Џ џ	–	–	dzh
37	Ш ш	shah	Ш ш	Ш ш	Ш ш	Ш ш	Ш ш	Ш ш	sh
38	Щ, щ,	shchah	Щ ш	Щ щ	–	– –	Щ[6] щ[6]	–	shch[6]
39	(Ъ)¹ ъ	tverdy znak	(Ъ)¹ ъ	–	–	–	(Ъ)¹ ъ	–	"
40	(Ы)¹ ы	yerry	(Ы)¹ ы	–	(Ы)¹ ы	–	–	–	y
41	(Ь)¹ ь	myakhky znak	(Ь)¹ ь	(Ь)¹ ь	(Ь)¹ ь	–	–	–	'
42	Э э	eh	Э э	Є[7] є[7]	Э э	–	–	–	є[7]
43	Ю ю	yoo	Ю ю	Ю ю	Ю ю	–	Ю ю	–	yu
44	Я я	ya	Я я	Я я	Я я	–	Я я	–	ya
		TOTAL LETTERS	32[8]	32	33	30	29	29	

NOTE:

1 Letters in parentheses are ordinarily not found at the beginning of a word. Therefore, the capital form is used only when the entire word is capitalized.

2 Names of letters vary in different languages. Those given are primarily the Russian names in transliteration.

3 Scholars do not agree on a standard key for transliterating Cyrillic characters into English. The system presented here is a compromise without use of diacritical marks. Regarding divergent views on transliteration of Russian see *Science*, CXXIX (1959), 1111-1113, and CXXX (1959), 482-488.

4 Transliterate the Ukrainian and Byelorussian letter "h."

5 Transliterate the Ukrainian letter "e."

6 Transliterate the Bulgarian letter "sht."

7 Transliterate the Ukrainian letter "ye."

8 In the Russian alphabet, letter #9 (ё) is not counted as a separate letter.

9 Transliterate the Ukrainian letter "y."

TABLE III WRITTEN FORM OF SOME TYPICAL SLAVIC PHONEMES[1]

EASTERN			WESTERN				SOUTHERN					Trsl.	Approx. Engl. Equivalent
Russ.	Ukrain.	Byelor.	Polish	Czech	Slovak	Lusat.	Serb.	Croat.	Bulgar.	Sloven.	Maced.		
Дь	Дь	Дь	-	ď[5]	ď[5]	dj	ђ	đ	Дь	dj	-	dy	did you
Ж	Ж	Ж	(rz[2], ż, ż, zi)	(ř[2])ž	(ř[2],ž)ž	(řᵢ[2],ž)	Ж	ž	Ж	ž	Ж	zh	azure
Ль	Ль	Ль	-	-	l[5]	l[5]	Љ	lj	Ль	lj	Љ	ly	million
Нь	Нь	Нь	ń	ň	ň	ń	Њ	nj	Нь	nj	Њ	ny	canyon
Ть	Ть	Ть	-	ť[5]	ť[5]	tj	ħ	ć	Ть	tj	-	ty	hit you
Х	Х	Х	ch	ch	ch	ch	Х	h	Х	-	Х	kh	loch
Ц	Ц	Ц	c, ci, cz[3]	c	c	c, ć[4]	Ц	c	Ц	c	Ц	ts	its
Ч	Ч	Ч	ć, ci, cz[3]	č	č	č	Ч	č	Ч	č	Ч	ch	chain
-	-	-	dź, dż, dzi[3]	-	-	dž	Џ	dž	-	-	-	dzh	jump
Ш	Ш	Ш	ś, si, sz[3]	š, š	š, š	š, s[4]	Ш	š	Ш	š	Ш	sh	ashes
Шт	Шт	Шт	szt	št	št	št	Шт	št	Щ	št	Шт	sht	ash tray
Щ	Ш	-	szcz	šč	šč	štš	-	štš	-	štš	-	shch	fresh cheese

NOTE: [1] All correspondences are approximations.

[2] The *r* variations are close fusions of *r* and *zh* or *sh*.

[3] Where more than one rendition is given, slight differences exist but are not important enough to warrant separate entries.

[4] The first is hard, the second soft.

[5] The inverted circumflex is sometimes placed on top or abbreviated to an apostrophe.

1.7. Albanian

Albanian (self-designation *shqip*), thought to be the descendant of ancient *Illyrian,* constitutes the smallest grouping of the Indo-European family. It is spoken by almost 3 million people, of whom 1,900,000 live in Albania and the rest in Yugoslavia, southern Italy, Sicily, Greece, and the United States, mainly in New York City and Boston. There are two main dialects, which show considerable differences but are mutually intelligible. The Tosk dialect spoken in the south of Albania serves as the official language of the country; the Gheg dialect is spoken in the north.

Literature goes back to the fifteenth century. The Latin alphabet is used without the *w* but with *ç* and *ë* added to express the *ch* sound as in 'church' and the *o* umlaut respectively. In the Gheg dialect, the latter sound is written like the Cyrillic є . Albanian also has the *u* umlaut, written as *y*. The dental spirants are written *dh* for the voiced and *th* for the voiceless. The only accent used is the circumflex to indicate that a vowel is strongly nasalized. It is used sparingly and occurs more often in the Gheg dialect.

There are two genders, masculine and feminine. The definite article, *i* for masculine singular, *a* for feminine singular, *t* for the plural, is always suffixed, as in *mal,* "mountain," *mali,* "the mountain," *male,* "mountains," *malet,* "the mountains." The noun declension has three cases; the conjugation has a rich inflectional system. Interrogative and negative forms use special prefixes. The vocabulary has many loanwords from Latin, Turkish, Greek, and Bulgarian.

1.8. Armenian

The bulk of the over 4 million speakers of Armenian (self-designation *hayeren*) is located in the USSR. There, the Armenian SSR has 2 million and the Georgian and Azerbaijan SSR each have another 500,000 speakers of Armenian. In addition to these 3 million on Russian soil, there are settlements amounting to 300,000 each in the adjacent districts of Iran and Turkey, and also in Syria. Egypt and Lebanon account for 100,000 each. Smaller Armenian communities are found throughout the Middle East and the Balkan countries. There are about 100,000 Armenian speakers in the United States, concentrated in eastern coastal towns and cities.

The classical form of the language, still used in the service of the Armenian church, is known as *Krapar*, in contradistinction to the modern form, *Ashksarhik*, which evolved in the sixteenth century. There are two major divisions, the East Armenian which is the language used within the USSR, and the West Armenian which is spoken primarily outside the Soviet Union. The latter shows the effect of a medieval soundshift, a phenomenon similar to the Germanic Soundshift.

In order to translate the Bible from Greek, a missionary, Mesrop, invented around A.D. 400 thirty-six of the thirty-eight characters of the Armenian alphabet, patterning them on Iranian and Greek letters. He thus made the Bible accessible to his fellow-countrymen who were forbidden by their Persian rulers to read Greek.

Armenian is analytic and agglutinative. It has no grammatical gender. The definite article, *e* or *n*, depending on whether the noun ends in a consonant or vowel, is suffixed. Noun declension has seven cases; the plural ending is *er*. The conjugation shows many forms; passive and reflexive are formed by an infix, *u*. The vocabulary shows influences from Turkish and Persian.

1.9. Indo-Iranian Group

The easternmost group of the Indo-European family includes more individual languages than any other group, about one

hundred. Indo-Iranian languages also represent the block
with the largest total number of speakers, about 470 million,
who are located in one of the world's fastest growing centers
of population. Official languages of six countries belong to
this group. It may be subdivided into an eastern, Indic, subgroup native to India, Pakistan, Nepal, and Ceylon; and a
western, Iranian, subgroup extending from West Pakistan to
Afghanistan, the USSR, Iran, Iraq, Turkey, and Syria. Speakers of Indic languages total 430 million; those of Iranian, 40
million. The name *Aryan* is sometimes applied to the Indo-
Iranian languages or to the entire Indo-European language
family.

INDIC SUBGROUP

Almost all Pakistanis and Nepalese, as well as four-fifths of
the inhabitants of India and the majority of Ceylonese, speak
an Indic language. After British rule ceased in 1947, India
and Pakistan were separated on the basis of religious consid-
erations. The administrative entities of predominantly Hindu
India, now estimated to have 472 million inhabitants, were
consolidated out of the patchwork of princely realms into
states whose borders divided different speech communities. In
predominantly Moslem Pakistan, with an estimated population of 100 million, *Urdu,* the principal language of the west,
and *Bengali,* that of the east—separated from each other by
nine hundred miles of Indian territory—were declared, along
with English, official languages of the new country. Urdu had
arisen in the multilingual Mogul army camps of the sixteenth
century. The word *Urdu,* originally Turkish, meant "army"
and is the cognate of the English word "horde." The language
of an Islamic people, it is written with Arabic characters, supplemented by four letters to fulfill its linguistic requirements.
Urdu is a variant of *Hindi,* the main language of India, which
is written in its own version of the so-called Devanagari alpha-

bet. The name Pakistan means in Urdu "Land of the Pure,"
formed from *pak,* "spiritual purity," and *stan,* "land." The
letters of the name of the country also stand for its constituent
parts: P for Punjab, A for Afghan regions, K for Kashmir,
I for Islam, S for Sind, and TAN for the last syllable of Baluchistan.

Both Urdu and Hindi are often subsumed under the one
name of *Hindustani,* a name also used for one dialectical variant. The difference between Hindi and Urdu lies largely in the
vocabulary and form of writing; Urdu contains more elements
from Arabic and Persian, while Hindi makes a conscious effort
to perpetuate the older Indic word stock. Hindi is spoken by
165 million people in India, primarily in Uttar and Madhya
Pradesh, in the north central part of the country. It comprises
some varying tongues that are considered sufficiently similar to
be included, like *Bihari,* spoken by 30 million people in the
northeastern state of Bihar, and *Pahari,* with 2 million speakers near and in southern Nepal. With Urdu spoken by 20 million, mainly in Pakistan, the Hindi-Urdu combination is used
by 185 million speakers and thus constitutes the third most
widely spoken language in the world.

Bengali, the language of Rabindranath Tagore, 1913 winner
of the Nobel Prize for literature, is spoken by 47 million people in East Pakistan and 37 million in the adjoining Indian
state of West Bengal, of which Calcutta is the capital. *Punjabi*
is spoken in the Punjab territories in India (17 million) and
Pakistan (20 million), where one of the main dialects is
Lahnda. *Marathi,* spoken by 35 million people, is the language
of the Indian state of Mahrashtra, of which Bombay is the
capital, and *Gujarati,* Gandhi's language, with 22 million
speakers, is spoken in the Gujarat state. Bordering on it is the
Pakistani region where *Sindhi* is spoken by 4 million people.
The languages of the state of Rajasthan, spoken by 15 million
people, are grouped as *Rajasthani* and include *Marwari,* with
5 million speakers, *Jaipuri* and *Mewari,* each with 2 million
speakers, and *Bagri,* with 1 million speakers. It is anticipated

that these idioms will eventually coalesce with Hindi, and therefore they have not been among the languages specified in the Indian constitution.

In the northeastern section of India, *Assamese* is spoken by 6 million people in Assam, and *Oriya* is spoken by 15 million in the state of Orissa. *Nepali* has 7 million speakers in Nepal and over 1 million in the adjoining part of India and Sikkim. *Bhili* is spoken by 1 million in an enclave between the Marathi, Gujarati, and Rajasthani territories, and *Kashmiri*, with 2 million speakers, is divided between India and Pakistan. Sizable settlements of Hindi-speaking people are found abroad, notably on Mauritius and the Fiji islands; Gujarati is also spoken in eastern African countries.

One Indic language is spatially isolated from the others because an entirely different family, Dravidian, occupying the Deccan, is intercalated (See Chapter 6). This idiom is *Sinhalese,* spoken by 8 million people, or 70 percent of all Ceylonese, in and around the capital of Colombo in the southwestern part of the island-country of Ceylon, and on the Maldive Islands. Records exist from the last centuries B.C. The literary, "pure," form is named *Elu,* the colloquial form *Sinhala,* from the Sanskrit word for Ceylon.

The language of the Gypsies, *Romany,* is spoken by almost 1 million people, who live mainly outside India. Its linguistic separation from other Indic languages dates from the fifth to tenth centuries. Gypsies, so named from the mistaken belief that they came from Egypt, wandered into Europe between the ninth and the fifteenth centuries and are now concentrated mainly in Spain, Hungary, and other East European countries. The purest form of Romany is preserved in Hungary, but the language is heavily interlarded with elements from the surrounding local idioms.

Modern Indic languages have undergone considerable changes from Sanskrit. Phonemic peculiarities include cacuminal consonants, thought to be of Dravidian substratal origin, aspirated and nonaspirated pairs of stops, and vowel nasalization. Grammatical changes are analytic in the direction of simplification of inflections in nouns and verbs. Of the original three genders and eight cases of the noun declension, two genders, masculine and feminine, and two cases, nominative and oblique, remain. There are postpositive particles, and the verb is placed at the end of the sentence.

With the exception of Urdu, which as the language of an Islamic people is written with Arabic characters, the northern Indic languages employ variant forms of a common alphabet called *Devanagari,* meaning "God's language." This was already used for Sanskrit and may have been derived from a north Semitic writing in the eighth century B.C. Devanagari reads from left to right and has fourteen vocalic and thirty-five consonantal characters. Each consonant carries inherently with it a successive short *a* sound; other vowel values, nasalization, and aspiration are indicated by separate symbols or diacritical marks above, below, before, or after the consonants. The older Devanagari had almost five hundred ligatures, but the modern trend is to use not more than one hundred fifty. Bengali writing deviates more than the others from the original Devanagari and arose from it around A.D. 1100. The Sinhalese characters show similarities to the Dravidian alphabets. Romany has no written form except for Bible translations in Roman or Cyrillic characters.

The Indian constitution of 1950 recognizes fourteen languages of the country: ten Indo-European (Assamese, Bengali, Gujarati, Hindi, Kashmiri, Marathi, Oriya, Punjabi, Sanskrit, Urdu) and four Dravidian (Kanarese, Malayalam, Tamil, and Telugu). These are spoken by a total of 91 percent of the population. Twenty-three tribal languages are spoken by 12 million people, and there are about a hundred additional tongues, some with almost 1 million speakers. The 1951 census listed 782 different idioms without attempting to distinguish between languages and dialects or to weed out synonymic duplications. Nevertheless, the number of linguistic splinter groups is impressive.

IRANIAN SUBGROUP

The Iranian subgroup comprises *Persian* (self-designation *farsi*), spoken by 12 million people in Iran and 3 million in Afghanistan; *Pashto,* with 8 million speakers in Afghanistan and 6 million in West Pakistan; *Baluchi,* spoken by 1 million in Baluchistan, a southern part of West Pakistan, and 100,000 in Iran; *Tadzhik,* spoken by over 1 million in the Tadzhik SSR; and *Kurdish,* spoken in Kurdistan, an unofficial designation for a region situated mainly in eastern Turkey, northern Iraq and Iran, but extending into smaller adjoining sections of the USSR and Syria. Estimates of the number of the nomadic Kurds vary considerably, ranging from 3 to 15 million; perhaps 5 million speak the language natively, but many are bilingual. Most of them, possibly 2 million, are in Turkey, 1½ million in Iran, and 1 million in Iraq. A variant of Old Persian, *Avestan,* in which the Zend-Avesta, sacred literature of Zoroastrianism, was written, is still used liturgically.

The Iranian languages are written in Arabic letters supplemented and adapted to their particular phonemic needs, with the exception of Tadzhik which has a Cyrillic alphabet. The old form of Persian of the fifth century B.C. is preserved in cuneiform inscriptions.

ANCIENT WRITING

The name *Sanskrit,* or *Old Indic,* is applied to the ancient representative of the Indic languages. Certain features of the old Indo-European speech are preserved better in Sanskrit than in other Indo-European languages, like Greek or Latin. Its oldest form is known as *Vedic,* or *Vedic Sanskrit,* because it is the language in which the Vedas were written. These four sacred books of the Brahman religion are collections of hymns, prayers, and magic formulas. They may possibly go back as

far as the fifteenth or twentieth century B.C. The word *veda*
means knowledge.

By the fifth century B.C., Sanskrit, now known as Classical
Sanskrit, had become the secular literary language of India, and
its grammatical rules were fixed, largely through the efforts of
Panini. It ceased to be a spoken tongue, but its literary period
extended to about A.D. 1000. It is still used for liturgical purposes, and in the priestly hierarchy it is handed down through
generations. The last Indian census lists 1000 persons as speaking Sanskrit. Though not a vernacular, it is listed among the
fourteen languages recognized in India's constitution out of
reverence. The modern languages evolved after A.D. 1200 from
the early "Prakrits," meaning "vernaculars." Akin to them is
the older *Pali,* the speech of Buddha, which is still the liturgical language of Buddhism in Ceylon, Burma, and Thailand.

The numerals we know as Arabic are of Indian origin and
were invented by Hindu scholars nearly two thousand years
ago. The use of the place system by the Hindu numerals was
a great advance over the Greek system of assigning numerical
values to letters. The numerals became known in Baghdad
where in 825 a learned Arab, al-Khwarizmi, extolled their vir-
tues, launching them on their westward march. By the tenth
century, they had reached Spain and by the twelfth century,
central Europe, yet suspicion and prejudice against this pagan
innovation delayed general adoption until the fifteenth century. The numerals now used by eastern Arabs agree with our
so-called Arabic figures only in the 1 and 9, because each pattern has experienced gradual alterations through the centuries.

2. CAUCASIAN LANGUAGES

The northern and southern slopes of the Caucasus Mountains are, or were, the home of a language family that at one time was much more extended and the offspring of which may, like Basque, be remnants of pre-Indo-European languages. Some scholars, in fact, see a kinship between Basque and Caucasian, especially the northern groups, and label such a super-grouping *Japhetic*. There are about twenty-five living Caucasian languages, spoken by an aggregate of 5 million people. They may be conveniently divided into a northern branch of about twenty languages with 2 million native speakers and a southern of four languages spoken by about 3 million, although a family kinship between the two groups is doubted by Soviet linguists.

The northern group shows considerable diversification. Toward the east, *Chechen* is spoken by 400,000 in the Checheno-Ingush SSR. In remote valleys of the eastern mountain regions of Dagestan, there is a sizable number of different languages spoken by fewer than 10,000 people each, some by fewer than one thousand. In the western region, *Abkhaz* is spoken by 70,000 people in the Abkhazian ASSR. *Kabardin,* spoken by 200,000 in the Kabardinian ASSR, is the most important. Closely related is *Circassian,* which is spoken by 100,000 in the Cherkess ASSR and in scattered localities in Turkey and Syria, where the Cherkess people migrated around 1865 with several other language groups when their home territory became Russian. Many of the migrant stock have adopted the Turkish

language. Kabardin and Circassian are often combined under
the name *Adyge*. However, this name is sometimes used for
Circassian alone. More confusing is the fact that the 1959
USSR census shows separate counts for Kabardin, Circassian,
and Adyge.

Among the four languages belonging to the southern branch,
Georgian is the most important of all Caucasian tongues. Its
speakers, fewer than 3 million, live in the Georgian SSR and
adjoining parts of Azerbaijan and Turkey. Georgian, the
mother tongue of Stalin, developed from the speech of the
ancient Colchians. The first part of its self-designation *k'art'-
veli* may be traced to it, and the term means "land of Colchis."
Georgian has an old and rich indigenous literature, written
down since the fifth century in its own two alphabets, the
Chuzuri, "church writing," said to have been created by Mesrop, the inventor of the Armenian alphabet, and the *Mchedruli*, "war or secular script." The latter alphabet, completely
phonetic and consisting of forty symbols, is still in use although the Cyrillic alphabet is replacing it more and more.

Caucasian languages are generally agglutinative and inflecting, the declensional system being especially elaborate in the
northern group. There is no article. Northern Caucasian languages have numerous velar and laryngeal consonants. Semantic differentiation may result from affrication and lengthening
of consonants. Nouns are arranged according to classes whose
number varies from two to six. Intransitive verb forms pre-
dominate. Southern Caucasian languages have no diphthongs.
Words tend to end in a vowel; initial phonemes often include
imposing consonant clusters like *msxv* or *mch*, as evidenced by
the name of the Mchedruli script.

3. BASQUE

The *Basque* language (self-designation *euskara*) is native to the terrain on the Gulf of Biscay extending from Bilbao to Biarritz through part of four northern provinces of Spain and the adjoining territory of France. Of its 800,000 speakers, 700,000 live in Spain and the remainder in France; most of them are bilingual. The only sizable migration is to the United States, where the Basques' skill as shepherds makes them welcome in the West.

This is the only language in Europe that cannot be linked with any other European tongue; no attempt to establish a kinship with other languages, such as the Semito-Hamitic or Caucasian families or the extinct Etruscan, has ever been successful. A legend claims that the Basques are descended from Tubal, fifth son of Noah's son Japheth, who came to Europe before the Tower of Babel was built. He is said to have transmitted to his descendants the tongue spoken by Adam in the Garden of Eden. It is likely that Basque developed from an earlier Aquitanian or Iberian idiom which, before the Roman conquest, occupied a much larger area on the Iberian peninsula and the adjoining territory, later to become France. Thus it may well be the only remnant of tongues indigenous to Europe before the arrival of the Indo-Europeans. Basque place names can be traced back to the eighth century; the first book in the language dates from 1545.

The Basques, who call themselves *Euskaldunak,* are credited with having improved an ancient Mexican handball game, thought to have been imported by Cortés, and renamed it *jai alai,* meaning "merry festival."

The language is agglutinative and polysynthetic, building words by affixing and compounding. The definite article *a* is suffixed, as are the plural suffix *k* and other particles indicating noun functions. *Gizon,* "man," forms *gizona,* "the man," *gizonak,* "the men," *gizonakaz,* "with the men," and the like. A single entity may carry the concept of a phrase or sentence: *etcheradinokoan,* "going to my house," a structure derived by adding five suffixes to the root for "house." The conjugation abounds in inflectional endings, the verb incorporates both object and subject pronouns, and the syntax is very complex. The sentence "the book which I have given to the child is very pretty" would be rendered by *aurrari eman diodan liburua cil ederra da,* where the parts mean literally "child the to given I have which book the very pretty is."

There are a number of very divergent dialects which may be grouped under Biscayan, around Bilbao, and an eastern group, mainly Guipuzcoan, around San Sebastián. Basque phonemes include the Spanish guttural *j* sound and a large number of diphthongs. A modern text, especially if written in the Guipuzcoan form, can usually be identified by the profusion of *k, x, z,* the *ñ,* and several unusual combinations of two or three vowels.

4. SINO-TIBETAN LANGUAGES

The location of the speakers of Sino-Tibetan languages, the world's second-largest language family, is Central and Southeast Asia. Nine-tenths of this family belong to the Sinitic branch, the rest to the Tibeto-Burman. It is difficult to give accurate figures of speakers for the languages spoken within the People's Republic of China because its exact population is unknown, and for political reasons some authorities seem deliberately to underestimate the size of the population. The figure of 730 million in mainland China is probably closest to the truth; they speak a number of languages some of which do not even belong to this family.

What is commonly referred to as *Chinese* is in reality a complex of five major and some minor mutually unintelligible languages and dialects of disproportionate numerical ratios. By far the most important is the standard *Chinese-Mandarin* which since the beginning of the communist government in 1949 has been named *kuo yu,* or *kuan hua,* "national tongue." It is the speech of the inhabitants of north and central China and was the language of the imperial court at Peking, which means "northern capital," as opposed to Nanking, "southern capital." (Outside mainland China, the preferred form is Peiping, "northern peace," coined during the days of the republic before the advent of the communist regime.) This Mandarin-speaking zone is subdivided into northern (including Pekingese), southwestern, and southern Mandarin, and covers nine-tenths of mainland China, where three-fourths of all Chinese live. It does not include the speech of the western and extreme southern provinces nor the populous southeastern coastal strip. Nevertheless, Mandarin serves as official and superimposed legal and commercial language for both the People's Republic and Nationalist China. It is also one of the five languages of the United Nations. Over 515 million people speak Chinese-Mandarin; that is almost twice as many as speak English. Comparison of this figure with the world population of 3,225 million shows that nearly every sixth person on earth speaks Chinese-Mandarin. The annual population growth is 2.8 percent, much higher than the world average of 2 percent, so that in projecting the number of speakers of this language in the future it is necessary to add 14 million per year, or 25 persons every minute.

Wu is spoken by over 55 million in the Shanghai area and in Chekiang province. South of it, in Fukien, the language is *Fukienese* (self-designation *min*). Its more than 50 million speakers include 36 million on the mainland, 9 million on Taiwan, and 7 million in Southeast Asia, mainly Indonesia, Malaya, Singapore, the Philippines, and Borneo. *Cantonese* (self-designation *yueh*) has a total of 55 million speakers, 46 million of whom are in China's extreme southern provinces, Kwangsi and Kwangtung; the capital of the latter is Canton, officially known as Kwangchow. There are over 8 million speakers of Cantonese in Hong Kong, Thailand, Vietnam, Burma, and Cambodia, and nearly all Chinese in the United States speak it. Between the Mandarin, Fukienese, and Cantonese speech areas is a land-locked enclave where *Hakka*, a mixture of the other three, is spoken by 20 million. Its territory is the northeastern part of Kwangtung and the southern part of Kiangsi provinces.

Among the principal languages of the Tibeto-Burman branch are three national tongues, *Thai*, formerly known as Siamese, spoken by a total of 24 million in Thailand, the Yunnan province of China, and Viet Nam; *Burmese*, spoken by 18 million people in Burma; and *Lao*, spoken by 1½ million in north

Laos. Until the occupation of Tibet by the Chinese in 1950, *Tibetan,* spoken by 7 million in Tibet, Bhutan, and Nepal, was also an official language. *Lolo* (self-designation *nesu*) is spoken by 3 million in the Chinese provinces of Szechwan and Yunnan, while another 3 million speak *Miao* in parts of the Kweichow and Hunan provinces. *Shan* is spoken by 2 million in northeast Burma and part of Yunnan province of China. A number of other languages, including some in the Indian state Assam, have fewer than 1 million speakers each.

Generally, the structure of the Sino-Tibetan languages is monosyllabic or isolating, that is, every word is a single invariable syllable. As the number of pronounceable syllables is limited (there are 420 in Chinese-Mandarin), many words of different meanings are pronounced the same way. Thus, the syllable *shi* may designate, among other things, "lion," "corpse," "house," "poetry," "ten," "swear," "die." The listener must recognize the connotation from the context.

The existence of so many homophones has led to the expediency of combining two words of related meaning to prevent ambiguity. There are dozens of classifiers that may be added to determine the particular interpretation of a root. One is applied to round objects like rings and coins, others to human beings, animals, articles of clothing, and so on. An illustration of an analogous process might be the English word *ash tree* where the addition of the word *tree* rules out the meaning of *ash* as residue of combustion. In Chinese, "to see" is *jien,* but there are over twenty meanings of this word with the same sound. In order to define the meaning unequivocally, a related word, *kan,* "to look," may be added, forming *kan jien,* which then can be understood only as "seeing." A literal translation of such synonym compounds into English would yield a reduplicating "look see" effect. Two words often combine without performing a classifying function to yield a composite concept from the semantic components. This is especially true in place names with specific connotations: Shanghai, "mountain sea," Hainan, "sea south," Taiwan, "terrace bay," Taipei, "terrace north," Chungkuo (Chinese for China), "middle country."

A further characteristic of these languages, semantic pitch accentuation, aids in distinguishing different meanings of what would otherwise be the same word. This unusual feature, used also in some Bantu languages, characterizes them as tonal. In contrast to other languages, where high, low, rising, and falling inflections are used to express emphasis and emotions, Chinese tones serve to change the meaning of the word. The number of tones varies according to the language. Burmese, for example, has three tones, Thai five, Cantonese nine, Chinese-Mandarin four: high level, rising inflection, slight fall followed by an immediate rise, and abrupt fall. Chinese *ma* with high-level pitch means "nurse," with rising inflection, "hemp," with fall and subsequent rise, "horse," with abrupt fall, "curse." Dictionaries and grammars may indicate the tone by the position of level or slanting lines or by musical notes; systems of diacritical marks or superscript numerals also exist for romanized transcriptions.

The concept of parts of speech is lacking. In the absence of morphological changes, syntax is most important, that is, grammatical relations are entirely dependent on the position of the word in the sentence. As the sound of *r* is wanting, lallation takes place in adaptations from other languages: the sound is replaced by *l*.

Chinese writing is a cumbersome collection of about fifty thousand characters that are mainly ideograms without relation to the sound. However, some characters have come to be used for their phonetic value alone, and often a portion of the character serves as a phonetic symbol, imparting the sound to the whole character. This system, unique in the history of writing, originated more than four thousand years ago and is often credited with giving cohesion to the huge Chinese empire of different speech communities, for even though the spoken languages cannot be mutually understood, the written form, representing ideas only, is common to all. Thus, the word for "man" may be pronounced quite differently according to the language, but the written symbol is the same. Such a system of writing is comparable to musical notation or chemical and mathematical formulas, which convey the same meaning to all people even though they may be read with a different pronunciation.

There is a legend that Emperor Fu Hsi about 2900 B.C. invented a set of straight and broken lines to replace the knotted cords that were used for communications. A later emperor ordered a scholar named Tsang Chieh to improve this system, and hundreds of additional characters were devised, allegedly inspired by the marks of birds' feet in the sand. The oldest Chinese writing preserved is of the fourteenth century B.C. Since then, the shape of the characters has changed considerably, and as many as eight different period styles can be discerned. A comparison of early and late forms reveals that the earlier characters were more detailed pictures. However, while it is easy to identify some symbols, such as a crescent for "moon," a circle with a dot in the center for "sun," or a torso with two legs for "man," and surmise the origin of other similar simple characters, it is not possible in all cases to reconstruct the mental picture that led to the earlier forms because even these were already abbreviated.

Every symbol either is or contains in some shape one of two hundred fourteen keys or radicals that hint at the general idea of the class of objects to which it belongs; for example, all words relating to wood, like "tree" or "table," contain the "wood" radical. Words are indexed in the dictionary in the order of the radicals which in turn are lined up according to the number of strokes, from one to seventeen. It is self-evident that there are few men who can accomplish the formidable task of memorizing all the characters. Illiteracy is therefore widespread; only 20 percent of all Chinese have any knowledge of the script. A Chinese child learns about two thousand characters by the time he is ten; it takes at least six thousand symbols, the stock of an average newspaper, to be literate.

The presentation of abstract concepts like love, justice, democracy, communism, calls for some ingenuity. At times, signs for words with a similar sound are borrowed to provide a phonetic element that approximates the sound of the main term. An equivalent in English would be the use of the picture of berries to express the idea of "buries." Other solutions seem picturesque or facetious. Thus, the woman and child symbols combined mean "good"; "wife" is represented as a woman with a broom; a woman under a roof indicates "peace" but two women together means "quarrel." The symbols for "lightning" and "language" together yield the symbol for "telephone"; those for "words" and "tongue" together give "language."

Writing has traditionally been in vertical lines from right to left; however, some publications, especially in the People's Republic on the continent, now appear with writing running horizontally from left to right. In 1955, the People's Republic initiated a plan to simplify more than seventeen hundred characters, this number to be increased gradually so that over half of the most commonly used symbols would eventually be simplified. In 1956, a thirty-letter Latin alphabet including five variants for Chinese sibilant sounds was proposed for romanizing the script, but the chances for an early change from a system that enjoys the reverence of tradition and boasts alleged advantages in uniting different spoken tongues do not seem bright. For the present, the Latin alphabet will be used for annotating ideographs in dictionaries, also for indexing, telegraphy, and to show pronunciation of foreign names and technological terms.

Tibeto-Burman languages use their own alphabets, derived from the Indian Sanskrit of the seventh century A.D., when Tibetan was reduced to writing. It uses thirty-five basic symbols which form ligatures to express syllabic characters. The Burmese alphabet of eleven vowels and thirty-two consonants was derived from South India, probably in the eleventh century, and the Shan alphabet is a variation of it. In Burmese, tones and stresses are indicated by accents placed under or after the characters. Thai looks more angular and has forty-four consonant signs to which thirty-two vowel marks are added above, below, before, or after the consonants. Four of Thai's five tones are indicated by signs over the consonants, the absence of a sign implying the fifth tone. All of these scripts are written from left to right.

5. SEMITO - HAMITIC LANGUAGES

The name *Semito-Hamitic* is derived from Shem, Noah's eldest son, and Ham, his second son, thus reflecting the language group's greatest achievement, the Bible. It is believed that the shores of the Red Sea were the homeland of the speakers of these tongues. Their present territory extends from the Arabian Peninsula through the length of northern Africa to Mauritania and reaches as far north as the Caucasus and southward to the equator. The total of native speakers amounts to 125 million, but because of the religious importance of *Arabic* and *Hebrew,* and to a lesser degree *Coptic* and *Syriac,* many more people come into contact with languages of this family. It is divided into a Semitic branch with 100 million, and a Hamitic, with 25 million speakers. The latter is considered by some a separate language family.

5.1. Semitic Branch

ARABIC

The leading language of the Semitic branch is *North Arabic,* commonly referred to as *Arabic.* It is the native tongue of 29 million people in Asia and 62 million in Africa. Arabic is spoken by a majority of the population and has official status in the following seventeen countries, listed in the order of number of speakers of Arabic: Egypt, 28 million; Morocco, 10 million; Algeria, 9 million; Sudan, 8 million; Saudi Arabia, 7 million; Iraq, 6½ million; Yemen, 5 million; Syria, over 4 million; Tunisia, 3½ million; Lebanon and Jordan, over 1½ million each; Libya, 1 million; and with lesser numbers, Muscat and Oman, Kuwait, Bahrein, Trucial Oman, and Qatar. Arabic enjoys co-official status with Hebrew in Israel and with English in Malta. In three countries, Arabic is spoken by a large majority, but is not official. These are Aden and Chad, with over 1 million speakers each, and Mauritania, with 600,000. Sizable Arabic-speaking minorities are found in seven additional nations. Besides the 90 million native speakers, many more of the 450 million Mohammedans in the world have some knowledge of the tongue of the Koran, their sacred scripture and first extant Arabic literature, dating from the seventh century.

Arabic has a number of dialects which differ mainly in pronunciation and vocabulary; some diverge to such an extent that they are not mutually intelligible, but a standard Arabic, called *Fusha,* is used increasingly by the press and on the radio. The main dialects are Iraqi, Syrian, and Egyptian in the east, Saudi in the south, and Tunisian, Algerian, and Moroccan in the west. Maltese is an Arabic dialect that was greatly influenced by Italian; it is spoken by 200,000 Christians on the isle of Malta.

About 50,000 inhabitants of the central coast of Muscat and Oman and on the island of Socotra speak *South Arabic* which diverges from North Arabic so much that it is a distinct language. There are inscriptions in its ancient form dating from the ninth century B.C. Mahri and Socotri are the main dialects.

ETHIOPIC GROUP

The speakers of the Ethiopic languages descended from migrants to Africa from Yemen. Ethiopians derive their name from a Greek word meaning "burned faces." The primary and official language of Ethiopia is *Amharic,* spoken by 7 million people in and around the capital, Addis Ababa, and in an elongated area extending northward. *Ethiopic* proper (self-designation *ge'ez*) is no longer a spoken tongue and since the seventeenth century has been used only as a liturgical language of the Abyssinian Church; its modern descendant, *Tigrinya,* has 500,000 speakers in Eritrea, which became federated with Ethiopia in 1952. *Tigre* is spoken by 100,000 people on the Red Sea coast in northern Eritrea.

HEBREW

Hebrew is attested in inscriptions dating back to the ninth century B.C. The larger part of the Old Testament is written in this tongue. As a vernacular, Hebrew became extinct in the fourth century B.C. and for many centuries was used only in the Jewish religious service. After the establishment of the state of Israel, Hebrew (self-designation *ivrit*) was in 1948 declared the major official language of the country, with Arabic co-official. It is now the mother tongue of over 1 million speakers, or approximately two-fifths of the population of Israel, and in view of the stress that is laid on it as a national tongue, a rapid growth of the number of native speakers of modern Hebrew may be anticipated in the next generation. The revival of Hebrew as a spoken and written language after it had been dormant for over two thousand years is largely the result of the efforts of Eliezer Ben-Yehuda, who is credited with the invention of four thousand new Hebrew words. The enrichment and modernization of the vocabulary was accompanied by some grammatical innovations.

ARAMAIC - SYRIAC

Another Semitic tongue, *Aramaic,* which arose in the eighth century B.C., replaced Hebrew. At the time of Christ, it not only was the common language of all Jews, but also served as

an international medium throughout Palestine, Syria, Mesopotamia, even reaching as far as India. Small parts of the Old
Testament, the books Ezra and Daniel, as well as the Talmud
are written in it; *amen* and *hallelujah* are Aramaic words.
Beginning with the seventh century, this language, then referred to as *Syriac* after the location of most speakers, gradually gave way to Arabic under the proselytizing impact of the
Islamic religion, established in A.D. 622, though it maintained
itself into the seventeenth century in some sections of Lebanon.

Even today, about 4,000 inhabitants of the Syrian village of
Mahlula and of two neighboring settlements north of Damas-
cus speak a tongue very similar to that of Jesus, and an eastern
variant is spoken by a total of 200,000 people in several isolated communities in eastern Turkey, northern Iraq and adjacent Iran, the Armenian SSR, and on the Malabar coast of
southwest India. Armenian Syriac, with only 20,000 speakers,
is called *Aisor*.

A rich Christian religious literature developed in Aramaic
between the second and fourteenth centuries. The standardized text of the tenth-century translation of the Bible into
Syriac is known as Peshitta, "the simple." An Aramaic liturgy
is still used throughout the world by Nestorians, Maronites,
and adherents of some other eastern sects.

5.2. Hamitic Branch

Languages belonging to the Hamitic branch are spoken in north
and northeast Africa and include four major tongues: *Hausa,
Berber, Galla,* and *Somali.*

Hausa was until recently considered a Sudanic language, but
has now been proved to be more closely related to the Semito-
Hamitic family. With several smaller tongues, it forms the
Chadic group. As a native language, Hausa is spoken by 9
million, which include over 7 million in the North Territory
of Nigeria where Hausa is official, 1 million in Niger, and the

remainder in Cameroun, Togo, and Dahomey. Additional millions use the language as a lingua franca throughout the neighboring African lands. Hausa has a moderate semantic pitch to distinguish otherwise homophonic words; for example, *wuya* with a falling tone means "neck," with a rising tone, "difficulty."

Berber is spoken in several dialects by over 6 million descendants of the original Libyco-Berber population of North Africa, who have maintained their own language against successive invasions of Phoenicians, Romans, and Arabs. Inscriptions go back to the fourth century B.C. The main reason for the survival of Berber is that the women live in seclusion; Berber is handed down from mother to child, while the menfolk are usually bilingual. Berber speech territory is compact in parts of Morocco, Chad, and Niger. In the latter country, it is the language of the Tuaregs and is called *Tamachek* by them. Other centers are in pockets in Libya and Tunisia. Algeria has the largest Berber-speaking concentration with 2 million speakers, and the language is known as *Kabyle*.

Galla and Somali belong to the Cushitic group, named after Cush, eldest son of Ham. Galla (self-designation *oromo*) is spoken by 6 million people in southern Ethiopia and adjacent Kenya, Somali by 3 million in Somalia, southern Ethiopia, and French Somaliland.

Coptic had developed in the third century A.D. as a lineal descendant of ancient *Egyptian,* which became extinct in the seventh century. Coptic itself ceased to be spoken three hundred years ago and survives only in ecclesiastical use in the Coptic Church. This language, which derives its name from an Arabic word meaning "Egyptian," was used by Champollion when he deciphered the Rosetta Stone in 1822 and thus opened the way to the understanding of Egyptian hieroglyphics, in use from about 3400 B.C. to the sixth century A.D.

The outstanding structural feature of the Semito-Hamitic family is triliterality of word roots. They consist mostly of three consonants, and the insertion or omission of vowels—often not written and to be supplied by the reader—or the vocalization of consonants serves to create a set of verb and noun forms whose meanings are related to that of the root. Thus, the Arabic radical *KTB,* carrying a fundamental reference to writing, yields *KiTaBa,* "to write," *aKTuBu,* "I write," *KaTaBa,* "he wrote," *yaKTuBu,* "he will write," *yuKTaBu,* "it is written," *KuTiBa,* "it was written," *KiTaB,* "book," *KuTuB,* "books," *KaTiB,* "writer," *KaTBun,* "writing." Correspondingly, from Hebrew *KTV* are derived *KoTuV,* "written," *KTiVah,* "writing," *KTiV,* "spelling," *KToVet,* "inscription," *KTaV,* "script," *KaTaV,* "correspondent." The Arabic root *SLM* forms *SaLaM,* "peace," *iSLaM,* "submission" [to God], hence the name for the religion, and *muSLiM,* "submitting" [person], a Moslem. In most languages, consonants are the main carriers of thought, and an analogous principle may be observed in English abbreviations. In addition to the internal changes, there are also a few prefixes and suffixes. Syntactically, there is an isolating tendency to place words together without indication of the grammatical relationship.

Phonemic characteristics include the glottal stop and spirant, vocalism limited to three, and an unaccented neutral vowel called *schwa,* similar to the *e* in English 'quiet.' A rather large number of consonants includes velar spirants.

Arabic nouns have two genders, masculine and feminine; Hebrew has fewer declensional forms than Arabic. The definite article is *al* in Arabic and precedes the noun, and the indefinite article, *un,* is suffixed: *al malik,* "the king," *malikun,* "a king." Some English words, *alchemy, alcohol, algebra,* betray their Arabic origin in the first syllable. In Hebrew the definite article is *ha* and is prefixed to the noun.

Arabic writing is horizontal from right to left. Most of the twenty-eight letters have four variant forms depending on whether they are used in isolated position or as the initial, medial, or final letter of a word. Most of them combine to form many ligatures. Vowels are not usually indicated, but a system of marking them by certain symbols, a line or hook above or below the preceding consonant, is used in religious literature. When such marks are supplied, the absence of a vowel sound is indicated by a circle, *sukun*. Maltese and Socotri are written with a modified Roman alphabet.

The Ethiopic languages have their own script consisting of twenty-six consonantal symbols; vowels are designated by adding little hooks, lines, or circles. This results in a total of over two hundred syllabic characters. After the introduction of Christianity in the third and fourth centuries, the direction of writing from right to left was changed to run from left to right.

Hebrew has a twenty-two-character alphabet. Like the Arabic it developed from an older common Semitic form, Phoenician, which itself goes back to the Egyptian hieroglyphics. Five letters have different forms when used in a final position. The insertion of a point (*dagesh*) into three letters changes a spirant to a stop, and in one character the position of the superscript point differentiates between the *s* and *sh* sounds. As in Arabic, the direction of writing is from right to left, but the letters are not usually joined. Opening quotation marks are at the bottom of the line.

There is an older form, *Square Hebrew,* and a newer, more cursive style, *Rabbinical.* Very early, the defective unvocalized script was changed to the so-called *plene* form by making use of unpronounced consonantal signs to indicate the missing long vowel sounds. They are called *matres lectionis* and are used in common writings. In the Scriptures, vowels are indicated by the Masoretic points, so called because, between the sixth and eleven centuries, they were supplied by the Masoretes, scholars who determined the correct pronunciation of Biblical Hebrew following the *masora,* "tradition." They are dots and dashes placed below or after the preceding consonants; a dot under a consonant is like a short *i,* a dash, a short *o.* Only the Bible, children's books, and poetry indicate vowels in this manner.

Syriac writings run from right to left. The original script, *Estrangelo,* took its name from *satar,* "writing," and *evangelo,*

SQUARE HEBREW						ARABIC						
#	(letter)	final	name*	trsl.*	#	isolated	final	median	initial	name*	trsl.*	cf. Hebrew
1	א		alef	ʾ 1/	1	ا	ـا	-	-	alif	ʾ 9/	1
2	ב		vet	v 2/	2	ب	ـب	ـبـ	بـ	bah	b	2
3	ג		gimel	g	3	ت	ـت	ـتـ	تـ	tah	t	} 22
4	ד		dalet	d	4	ث	ـث	ـثـ	ثـ	thah	th	
5	ה		heh	h	5	ج	ـج	ـجـ	جـ	jeem	dzh 10/	3
6	ו		vav	v 3/	6	ح	ـح	ـحـ	حـ	hah 11/	h 11/	8
7	ז		zayin	z	7	خ	ـخ	ـخـ	خـ	khah	kh	
8	ח		Khet	kh	8	د	ـد	-	-	dal	d	} 4
9	ט		tet	t	9	ذ	ـذ	-	-	dhal	dh	
10	י		yod	y 4/	10	ر	ـر	-	-	rah	r	20
11	כ	ך	khaf	kh 5/	11	ز	ـز	-	-	zah	z	7
12	ל		lamed	l	12	س	ـس	ـسـ	سـ	seen	s	21
13	מ	ם	mem	m	13	ش	ـش	ـشـ	شـ	sheen	sh	
14	נ	ן	nun	n	14	ص	ـص	ـصـ	صـ	sad 11/	s 11/	18
15	ס		samekh	s	15	ض	ـض	ـضـ	ضـ	dad 11/	d 11/	
16	ע		ayin	ʿ 6/	16	ط	ـط	ـطـ	طـ	tah 11/	t 11/	9
17	פ	ף	feh	f 7/	17	ظ	ـظ	ـظـ	ظـ	zad 11/	z 11/	
18	צ	ץ	tsadee	ts	18	ع	ـع	ـعـ	عـ	ayn	ʿ	16

TABLE IV
SEMITIC ALPHABETS

SQUARE HEBREW				ARABIC							
#	name	trsl.		#	isolated	final	median	initial	name	trsl.	cf. Hebrew
19	qof	k		19	غ	غ	غ	غ	ghayn	kh	16
20	resh	r		20	ف	ف	ف	ف	fah	f	17
21	sin	8/		21	ق	ق	ق	ق	qaf	q [12/]	19
22	tav	t		22	ك	ك	ك	ك	kaf	k	11
				23	ل	ل	ل	ل	lam	l	12
				24	م	م	م	م	meem	m	13
				25	ن	ن	ن	ن	noon	n	14
				26	ه	ه	ه	ه	hah	h [13/]	5
				27	و	و	-	-	waw	w	6
				28	ي	ي	ي	ي	yah	y	10

NOTE:

*Spellings of names and transliterations are compromises of various systems.

1 Yiddish: *a, o.*
2 With dagesh: bet, transliterate *b.*
3 Yiddish: *u.*
4 Yiddish: *i.*
5 With dagesh: kaf, transliterate *k.*
6 Yiddish: *e.*
7 With dagesh: peh, transliterate *p.*
8 With superscript dot, ש sin, transliterate *s,* but שׁ shin, transliterate *sh.*
9 Do not transliterate initially.
10 Egypt: *g,* Syria: *zh.*
11 Often written with subscript or inscript mark.
12 Egypt: ء
13 With two superscript dots and before vowel, transliterate *t.*

"evangelist," and had vowels indicated by *matres lectionis*. The schisms dividing Syriac-speaking Christians created two new types of writing. In *Jacobite,* named after the sixth-century bishop Jacob Baradaeus, small Greek vowels are written above or below the consonants; in *Nestorian,* named after the fifth-century bishop Nestorius of Constantinople, vowels are indicated by dots and dashes. Russian Armenian Syriac uses the Cyrillic alphabet.

In the Hamitic branch, Hausa formerly used a modified Arabic writing, *Ajami,* but has changed to Roman letters. Berber is written with Arabic letters, except for the Tamachek variant, which has its own twenty-four-consonant alphabet, *Tifinagh.* Galla uses the Ethiopic script; Somali, Roman letters. Coptic had its own writing, derived from the Greek alphabet and supplemented by seven letters.

5.3. Ancient Writing

Akkadian was an East Semitic language spoken in Mesopotamia from about 2800 to the fourth century B.C. Its form up to 650 B.C. is known as *Assyrian;* after that date it is often referred to as *Babylonian.* Around 2500 B.C. the Akkadians adopted the syllabic cuneiform writing system from their southern neighbors, the Sumerians, although their languages were not related. The Sumerians had used this system possibly as early as 4000 B.C. and continued it until the language died in the second century B.C. Sumerian, therefore, was the first language to be written. Akkadians, and later the Persians, used cuneiform and improved it until it was abandoned. Originally written in vertical columns from right to left, it was later changed to run horizontally from left to right.

Thus, the Semito-Hamitic language family has advanced not only man's oldest known writing but also the various alphabets that serve the vast majority of all literate people in the world and that have been traced back to ancient Egyptian.

6. DRAVIDIAN LANGUAGES

The Dravidian family, representing about 120 million speakers, is believed to have descended from a uniform language spoken throughout the peninsula of India before the arrival of Indo-Europeans, sometime in the second millennium B.C. Dravidian tongues are now largely confined to the southern tip of India, the Laccadive Islands, and the northern and eastern coasts of Ceylon. Four of these languages are specified in the Indian Constitution: *Telugu*, spoken by 42 million people in Andhra Pradesh; *Tamil*, spoken by a total of 37 million, including 33 million in the State of Madras and 3 million in Ceylon; *Kanarese*, spoken by 17 million in Mysore; and *Malayalam*, spoken by 15 million in Kerala and on the Laccadives. There are 800,000 Tamil speakers situated in southern Malaya, smaller groups in Singapore and South Africa. In the southeastern corner of Madhya Pradesh, *Gondi* is spoken by 1 million in scattered localities north of the Telugu area. In an enclave in West Pakistan and Iran, *Brahui* is spoken by about 200,000 people. Tamil possesses the oldest and richest Indian literature, except for Sanskrit. Malayalam arose as a variant of Tamil.

Dravidian languages are characterized by cacuminals and a number of liquids. Verbs have affirmative and negative voices attained by suffixion. The pronoun has distinctive inclusive and exclusive first person plural forms to denote inclusion or exclusion of the person addressed, as in the sentence, *"we* invite you to *our* house where *we* [including *you*] will have a good time with *our* games." The gender of nouns distinguishes between superior and inferior beings, the latter including inanimate objects.

The Dravidian languages have individually distinctive alphabets, derived from a common ancestor akin to the Sanskrit writing. The characters form many ligatures. Although the alphabets are different and their letters have divergent phonetic values, the cursive forms show kinship. Tamil writing is somewhat more angular than the others. The same parent also produced the Sinhalese and Tibeto-Burman alphabets. Brahui and Gondi are written in Arabic and Devanagari respectively.

7. JAPANESE

Some linguists connect *Japanese* (self-designation *nihongo*) with *Korean* to form a Japanese-Korean language family, whereas others consider Korean a member of the Altaic branch of the Uralic-Altaic family. Until we have more insight into a possible generic kinship with other languages, it seems expedient to treat Japanese as a language unrelated to any other.

It is the native tongue of about 95 million people, most of whom inhabit the empire of Japan, named Nippon, "land of the rising sun," from *ni*, "sun," and *hon*, "origin." Other concentrations of Japanese speakers are found on the neighboring Ryukyu Islands and on Taiwan. Dialectical differentiation is insignificant.

The Japanese are thought not to be indigenous to the islands they now occupy though their precise origin is a mystery. There is no linguistic kinship between Chinese and Japanese, but the influence of the literature and philosophy of Chinese Confucianism led to the adoption of the Chinese writing system by the Japanese in the third and fourth centuries. Borrowing the script does not, of course, make the two languages related—Greek did not become a Semitic language by adopting the Phoenician writing.

Nowhere is the difference between Chinese and Japanese more apparent than in the phonemes and the structure of words. True Japanese words are polysyllabic and tend to become formidably long by a process of agglutination. Each syllable is open, that is, either constitutes a vowel or consists of a consonant followed by a vowel, *n* being the only consonant that may end a syllable or a word. When foreign words are borrowed, a neutral vowel is inserted into clusters of consonants to make the word acceptable, as in *bifusuteki,* "beef steak," or *sutoroberi keki,* "strawberry cake." Unlike Chinese, Japanese has no tonal pitch; unlike English, it has almost no syllabic accent; so Japanese words generally show equal stress on each syllable. Therefore, the language is sometimes designated as atonal.

Vowels have cardinal values but may be short or long. Written unstressed *i* and *u* are often not sounded, the latter especially at the end and in the verbal suffix *-masu.* Of the consonants, the *l* is lacking and is regularly replaced by *r* in loanwords. As the Japanese shows the direct opposite of the Chinese inability to pronounce *r* and consequent tendency to replace it by *l,* this feature was used during World War II in shibboleths like *Lallapalooza* to distinguish friend from foe. The *g* is often nasalized; *f* is a bilabial; *sh, ch,* and *ts* are treated as single consonants. Adaptations of foreign words follow sound, not spelling. The spoken language is easily identified by its even tone, absence of pitch even in questions, and by such typical sentence endings as *-des(u), -mas(u), -masen, -mash(i)ta,* and *-ka,* the interrogative particle.

Compared with other languages, Japanese has a moderate foreign element in its word stock. The numerals up to ten exist in two forms, one originally Chinese and the other polysyllabic Japanese (1 *ichi* or *hitotsu;* 2 *ni* or *futatsu;* 3 *san* or *mittsu,* 4 *shi* or *yottsu;* 5 *go* or *itsutsu*). Moreover, there are root changes depending on the class of things counted (as *ichiwa, ippon, itchaku* in speaking of a bird, pencil, and suit respectively). Chinese words that have been borrowed since the introduction of the script usually betray their origin by having only one syllable, like *cha,* "tea," though now meaning explicitly Japanese tea. The earliest European visitors, the Portuguese, contributed the words *pan,* "bread," *shabon,* "soap," and *tempura,* Japanese fried shrimp.

Within the last hundred years, after Admiral Perry's visit in 1852 established contact between Japan and the western world, several hundred words were borrowed from the English language, most of which were well established before the American occupation following World War II. Some words and expressions are connected with the game of baseball which has aroused much enthusiasm: *beisuboru, homu-ranna, suroboru, fauru.* Other English words that have entered the Japanese vocabulary relate mainly to food, clothing, and western objects that were previously unkown, as *naifu, foku, hankechi, kara, nekutai.*

Japanese grammar lacks many forms that Indo-European languages take for granted. There are no gender and no plural in nouns. Where needed, a distinction between singular and plural is made by adding another word or repeating the same one. There is no article: *hon* may mean "book," "the book," "a book, "books," or "the books." Nouns and pronouns are not declined; their syntactical relationship is indicated by particles following them. Adjectives are conjugated. Verbs are impersonal, indicating present or past tenses and mood, but not person and number, which have to be deduced from the context. They have special negative forms and are usually placed at the end of the sentence. The result is an elliptical and at times baffling sentence pattern, as exemplified by *Eigo ka Doitsugo ga wakaru hito wa imasen ka?* Literal translation: *Ei* — English; *go* — language; *ka* — either; *Doitsu* — German; *go* — language; *ga* — sign of subject; *wakaru* — understanding; *hito* — person; *wa* — as for; *imasen* — is not; *ka* — question mark. Meaning: Is there anyone who understands English or German?

A feature of Japanese is the use of honorific forms to an extent unequaled in other languages. This is a reflection of the Japanese code of courtesy, which may seem exaggerated by western views, but is one of the most charming characteristics of the people. Japanese etiquette requires stressing of the gulf between socially superior and inferior persons as an expression of politeness. As English does not share this aspect, an attempt to render the flavor of the Japanese in translation is frequently made by the addition of the adjective "honorable" or of such phrases as "you deign to" or "you condescend to." To be sure, western languages do not lack this feature completely, but depend on stylistic differences, special pronouns (French *tu* and *vous*), the attributive use of nouns (Spanish *su señor padre*), or certain words that can refer only to the person addressed and never to the speaker (German *Ihre Gemahlin*).

The Japanese language has many parallel sets of humble and polite words, especially in designating family relationships. Thus, the speaker's own father, mother, husband, wife would be named by him *chichi, haha, shujin,* and *kanai,* while he would refer to the same relatives of the person addressed as *otosama, okasama, goshujin,* and *okusan* respectively. The social distance is achieved not merely by different roots but also by characteristic affixes. Sometimes, the particle *o* serves as the honorific. In addition to the difference between the familiar and polite verbal endings, *u* and *imasu* respectively, there are completely different honorific roots. The verb for "I give" is *ageru,* literally "I offer up," whereas "you give" is *kudasaru,* literally "you hand down." "To go" is *mairu, iku,* or *irascharu,* that is, humbly, as an equal, or respectfully. In addition, verbs change their endings according to the degree of politeness toward the person addressed or discussed.

The Japanese adopted the Chinese characters around A.D. 300. As these are ideographic without relation to the pronunciation, Japanese, as well as any other language, can be written entirely in this script, *kanji.* Obviously, knowledge of a large number of symbols is required. One Japanese dictionary contains twenty-five thousand. In 1947, a list of eighteen hundred fifty essential characters was drawn up and approved as the only ones to be used henceforth.

In the eighth century some *kanji* symbols were simplified to create two syllabaries, *kana,* to render sounds phonetically, such as *ka, ki, ku, ke, ko.* The *katakana,* more angular, is preferred for signs, formal documents, foreign names, and children's books; the *hiragana* is more cursive and is used more commonly. The two styles may be compared to English printing and script though the difference between the two *kana* syllabaries is greater.

Each *kana* consisted originally of forty-eight syllables in addition to one symbol for *n,* but is now reduced to a total of forty-six. These may be arranged as the five vowels *a, i, u, e, o,* with succeeding rows formed by a preceding *k, s, t, n, h, m, y, r, w.* Voiced consonant syllables are indicated by adding two dots called *nigori* to the unvoiced symbols and the *p*-range may be formed from the *h*-range by adding a small circle called *maru* or *handaku.*

Even after it developed that all Japanese words could be written entirely in *kana,* the Chinese ideographs were not discarded; *kana* is used in conjunction with them, mostly to indicate word endings and connecting particles, as adverbs, postpositions, conjunctions, and interjections. *Kana* thus written alongside the ideographs is called *furigana* and is often found in newspapers and books to designate the pronunciation of the *kanji.* The modern tendency is to intersperse *kana,* this mixture being named *kana-majiri.*

Japanese can also be written with Roman letters called *romaji.* There are three systems of romanization, the Hepburn, Nippon, and Kunrei styles. In the Hepburn system the macron is used to indicate long *a, u, e, o,* but the long *i* is rendered as *ii.* Transcriptions into alphabetical *romaji* are considered more difficult to read than the numerous *kanji* and *kana* symbols. For example, street addresses, if given in English or *romaji,* usually add the *kanji-kana* version for the benefit of the taxi drivers. A Japanese typewriter includes *kanji,* the two *kana* series, and *romaji,* a total of about four thousand characters.

It is possible, then, to write Japanese in eight different ways: *kanji* mixed with *hiragana, kanji* with *furigana* (lateral *katakana* or *hiragana*), pure *katakana,* pure *hiragana,* Hepburn *romaji,* Nippon *romaji,* and Kunrei *romaji.* Writing, as in Chinese, usually begins on the right at the top of the page and proceeds in vertical columns from right to left. Left-to-right horizontal writing is found in some scientific books, and public signs may run from right to left.

8. URALIC-ALTAIC LANGUAGES

The Uralic-Altaic family owes its name to the assumed original home of the speakers, the foothills of the Ural and Altai mountain ranges. The name *Turanian* is also applied to these languages and is derived from Tur, one of three brothers from whom, according to Persian legend, the races of mankind descended. The effect of medieval and later migrations is apparent in the vast expanse of the present area and in the phenomenon that not all languages are contiguous, their isolation having been caused mainly by intercalated Slavic tongues like Russian. The 90 million speakers now cover a territory extending from eastern Europe through the Russian heartland and Siberia to the Pacific Ocean. The family includes national languages of five countries and six constituent Soviet Republics.

Comprising 20 million speakers, the Uralic branch is divisible into three groups. One, the Finnic, spoken by 8 million people, includes *Finnish, Estonian, Mordvin,* and *Lapp.* Finnish (self-designation *suomi*) has 4 million speakers in Finland and sections of neighboring Carelia and Estonia. An additional 300,000 each live in the United States and Sweden, so that the total number of speakers approaches 5 million. The indigenous name of the country of Finland, "Suomi," is composed of the roots *suo,* "fen," and *maa,* "land," yielding the meaning: land of fens or marshes. Estonian (self-designation *eesti*) has about 1 million speakers and is linguistically closest to Finnish. Over 1 million speakers of Mordvin are located in the Mordovian ASSR, east of Moscow. Lapp (self-designation *sâme*) is spoken by 40,000 people, largely nomads, north of the Arctic Circle. Over half of them live in Norway, the others in Sweden and Finland.

The Ugric group contains mainly 12 million speakers of *Hungarian* (self-designation *magyar*), of whom about 9 million live in Hungary. Other Hungarian groups include the 1 million Szeklers who claim descent from the fifth-century Hun invaders and occupy an autonomous region in Transylvania, where Hungarian is co-official with Rumanian. There are 500,000 native Hungarian speakers in the United States and 500,000 in Yugoslavia, 400,000 in Czechoslovakia, 150,000 in the USSR, and smaller numbers in the Balkan countries. Hungarian has the oldest documents in any Uralic language, dating from the thirteenth century.

The third group, Samoyedic, is spoken by 25,000 people in northwestern Siberia near the mouths of the Ob and Yenisei rivers. The main language is *Samoyed,* with 22,000 speakers, Because Samoyed means "cannibal" in Russian, its speakers prefer to call their language *nenets.*

Altaic languages, with a total of 70 million speakers, may likewise be divided into three groups: Turkic, Mongolian, and Manchurian. In the Turkic group, comprising 65 million, *Turkish* (self-designation *türkçe*) is the most important. The bulk of the 27 million speakers of Turkish live in Turkey, and there are about 250,000 in Yugoslavia and 200,000 each in Bulgaria and Greece. Turkish is the only official language of Turkey; it is co-official with Greek in Cyprus, where the 110,000 speakers of Turkish constitute one-fifth of the population. *Azerbaijani* (self-designation *azeri*) is spoken by over 3 million people in the Azerbaijan SSR and by 4 million in northwestern Iran. *Uzbek* has 5 million speakers in the Uzbek SSR and an additional 2 million in neighboring Soviet republics and Afghanistan. *Tatar* (5 million) and *Chuvash* (1 million) are spoken at the bend of the Volga River near Kazan in the Tatar and Chuvash ASSR respectively. There are almost 5 million speakers of *Kazakh,* the bulk in the USSR and 600,000 in the Chinese province Sinkiang. *Kirgiz* (1 million) and *Turkoman* (over 1 million) are the main languages in the Kirgiz and Turkmen SSR respectively, with Turkoman overlapping into Afghanistan. *Uighur* is spoken by 4 million in Chinese Turkistan, the western part of Sinkiang, where it is the official language. A group of 80,000 speakers of Uighur is in the USSR, mainly in the Kazakh SSR.

The Mongolian group, with 2 million speakers, covers eastern Sinkiang, the Mongolian Republic, and parts of Chinese Inner Mongolia. The main language is *Khalkha,* or *Mongol* proper, with almost 1 million speakers. In Mongolia it is the official language; there is also a linguistic island inside of Chinese territory.

The Manchurian group, totaling 300,000 speakers, includes *Manchu* proper, spoken by 200,000 in scattered regions in northern Manchuria, and *Tungus* (self-designation *evenki*) with 15,000 speakers spread thinly over an enormous territory in eastern Siberia. Some scholars include Korean in the Altaic branch.

A high degree of agglutination and the principle of vowel harmony between suffix and root are the main characteristics of the Uralic-Altaic languages. Grammatical relations, including possessive pronouns, are expressed mainly by suffixion: *Budapesten,* "in Budapest." Word formation may be illustrated by the Hungarian derivation of *elad,* "sell," from *el,* "away," and *ad* "give," or *adhat,* "may give," from *ad* and *hat* "ability," or *eladhatatlan,* "inalienable," from *el, ad, hat,* and *atlan,* a negative particle. Similarly, in Turkish, the parts *el,* "hand," *im,* "my," *ler,* "plural," and *de,* "in" yield *ellerimde,* "in my hands"; in the verbal structure the root *gel,* "come," forms *gelmek,* "to come," *gelmemek,* "not to come," *gelebilmek,* "to be able to come," and *gelememek,* "to be unable to come." Nouns, adjectives, and numerals are declined, with endings highly diversified: Finnish and Estonian form as many as fifteen cases. Typical plural endings are *t* in Finnish,

d in Estonian, *k* in Hungarian, *ler* or *lar* in Turkish. The conjugation is also complex; the verb has special negative forms.

Vowel harmony requires that if the root has a front vowel,
like *ä, ö,* or *ü* (*y*), in some languages also *e* and *i,* all suffixes must contain front vowels; a back vowel, like *a, o, u,* or
Turkish undotted *i* (*ı*) must be followed by back vowels. For
example, if Finnish *pöly,* "dust," is to combine with *ssa,* the
suffix meaning "in," the resulting derivative is *pölyssä,* "in
the dust." Hungarian *kert* 'garden' and *ház* 'house,' form
the plurals *kertek* and *házak;* 'near the garden' is *a kertnél,*
but 'near the house' is *a háznál.*

There is no gender. Finnic and Altaic languages have no
article; in Hungarian, the article is *a* before a consonant and
az before a vowel. Stress is generally on the first syllable, but
long words have secondary stress; in Turkish, stress is rather
equally distributed over the syllables with a slight emphasis
on the last syllable.

Characteristic of Finnish and Estonian are the staggering
length of some words and the frequent doubling of consonants
and vowels to denote long sounds. Finnish has sixteen diphthongs. It lacks the letters *b, c, f, q, x, z.* Umlauts appear in print
as *ä* and *ö.* Estonian has three umlauts *ä, ö,* and *ü.* A tilde over
the *o* forms the symbol *õ* for a particular sound midway between *u* in 'rug' and *ur* in 'fur.' Hungarian uses the acute to
indicate lengthening of vowels. The *ö* and *ü* umlauts with
the usual two dots are short while a long sound is indicated
by slanting lines over the vowels: *ő, ű.* Hungarian is the only
language with this diacritical distinction.

The Uralic languages use Roman letters. The Altaic languages spoken in the Soviet Union, as well as Khalkha, have
recently adopted modified forms of the Cyrillic alphabet, but
those spoken outside the USSR usually employ Roman letters.
Uighur, Mongolian, and Manchu formerly had their own alphabets, which were kindred to each other and derived from
a Semitic writing. Uighur now uses Roman letters in China,
but Cyrillic in the small group across the border inside the

Soviet Union. Similarly, Kazakh is written in Cyrillic in the USSR, but the Roman alphabet was imposed by the Chinese in 1960 on the minority living in China. Eight new letters have been created to represent sounds peculiar to Kazakh and Uighur.

During the summer of 1928, Turkish converted from right-to-left Arabic to left-to-right Roman script, by decree of President Kemal Atatürk. The Turkish alphabet of twenty-nine letters omits *q*, *w*, and *x*, but includes for typical Turkish sounds an undotted *i* (*ı*) to denote the short vowel and a *g* with a breve over it to indicate the soft sound. A circumflex makes a vowel long. The *ö* and *ü* umlauts occur, and a cedilla under *c* and *s* indicates the *tsh* and *sh* phonemes respectively. Turkish spelling has no silent letters and is truly phonetic. In Estonian and Hungarian, opening quotation marks are placed at the bottom of the line.

9. OTHER ASIAN LANGUAGES

9.1. Southeast Asian Languages

The 45 million speakers of languages belonging to the Southeast Asian family live between the South China Sea and the heart of India. About twenty idioms exist, some in a compact territory, as in Viet Nam and Cambodia, some extending in scattered enclaves through Laos, Burma, Malaya, and India. Three distinct branches are constituted by *Vietnamese*, the Mon-Khmer, and the Munda languages.

Vietnamese has the largest number of speakers: 31 million. The majority, 17 million, live in North Viet Nam; there are 14 million in the southern Republic of Viet Nam. In both, Vietnamese has official status. There are two main dialects, the northern called Hanoi after the capital, and the other Saigon, after the southern capital. Vietnamese is spoken by small groups in Cambodia, Laos, and Thailand. Some linguists consider this language akin to Sinitic tongues with which it has some features in common. *Viet* is an ancient Chinese appellation for non-Chinese peoples, and *nam* is Chinese for "south," so that the country from which Vietnamese takes its name is called "Non-Chinese South."

Vietnamese, though probably originally agglutinative, is now an isolating tonal language. Its monosyllables consist of a vowel, diphthong, or triphthong which may be preceded and/ or followed by certain consonants. Words have as many as six tones that have a semantic function and may determine rad-

ically different meanings of the same word. There are a high
level, a high rising, a low falling, a low level, a falling, and
a level creaky tone, the last two accompanied by a closure of
the vocal folds. According to the tone used, the word *ma*
carries the meaning of "ghost," "cheek," "but," "rice seed-
ling," "grave," and "horse," respectively. Vietnamese thus
shows the structure and workings of an isolating language
more impressively than does Chinese. Vietnamese, too, uses
classifiers and synonym reduplication. Thought concepts are
obtained in joining words that convey the connotation of the
whole by combining those of the parts, as *mắt trời,* "eye
heaven," meaning "sun," or *xe lửa,* "vehicle fire," meaning
"train." In the absence of grammatical inflections, syntax is
very important, and the meaning of a sentence depends heavily
on word order.

Vietnamese uses the Latin alphabet. A breve may occur over
a, a circumflex over *a, e,* or *u.* Special letters are an *o* and *u*
with a lateral extension, *ơ* and *ư,* to indicate close sounds,
and a *d* crossed by a bar, *đ,* for the dental stop, to distinguish
it from ordinary *d,* which is a retroflex fricative. The high
rising tone is indicated by an acute, the low falling by a grave
over the vowel. The low level tone has a subscript dot. The
creaky tones are marked by a superscript *hamza* (*ʔ*) which is
vertical for the falling tone and horizontal, resembling a tilde,
for the level tone. The absence of any diacritic indicates the
high level tone.

The Mon-Khmer branch, with 8 million speakers, comprises
5 million speakers of *Cambodian* (self-designation *khmer*) in
Cambodia, where it is official, 300,000 speakers of *Mon* in
Burma east of Rangoon, and speakers of a dozen other languages, interspersed in southern Thailand and Laos, in Malaya, the Nicobar Islands, China's Yunnan Province, and
India's Assam. The Munda branch, composed of five languages
with a total of 5 million speakers, is located in three isolated
patches in central India with *Santali,* spoken by 3 million people in Orissa, as the chief language.

The Mon-Khmer and Munda languages are polysyllabic and agglutinative, preferably using infixes and suffixes. Cambodian and Mon have their own alphabets derived from Indian scripts; they in turn gave rise to the Thai, Lao, and Burmese alphabets. Texts run from left to right.

9.2. Korean

Korean (self-designation *chosenmal*) is the mother tongue of 37 million people in an area that is linguistically one of the most homogeneous in the world. There are 27 million in the Republic of Korea and 9 million in the People's Republic of Korea, between the 38th parallel and the Yalu River. The only sizable concentration of Korean speakers abroad is the 600,000 in Japan. Just as the geographical location of the Korean peninsula has for centuries furthered cultural cross-fertilization, so the language exhibits affinities to both Chinese and Japanese and reveals influences from west and east. The question of its linguistic kinship is unsettled, some scholars aligning it with Japanese, some with the Altaic group, others treating it as an unrelated entity.

Some phonemic features of the language are shared with Chinese and Japanese. Korean has both *l* and *r,* and *m* and *n* may occur in the final position. Bilabial fricatives are absent. The frequency of nasals is reminiscent of Chinese, but Korean does not have the tonal distinctions. Its syntax resembles Chinese; the precise function of each word in a sentence depends heavily on its position. Korean morphology shows similarities to Japanese. Nouns have no gender or plural forms; verbs have no conjugation. The word formation is agglutinative. A variety of roots and inflectional patterns provides the means for as many as six forms of civility to express a complicated differentiation of the social status of the person speaking, spoken of, or addressed.

Korean literature has existed since the seventh century. Chi-

nese characters were used for writing Korean until recent
times. Paralleling the Japanese *kana-majiri,* the *li-tu* system of
writing provides symbols for the phonographic rendition of
enclitics and suffixes. However, the trend is now toward the
use of the so-called *onmun* alphabet which was invented in the
fifteenth century. It consists of fourteen consonants and eleven
vowels with shapes derived from Chinese, Tibetan, and Sanskrit scripts. They are easily distinguished; all letters represent
invariable sounds and are grouped to form syllables where
every initial consonant is followed by its vowel. A final consonant is written underneath, and a special symbol precedes
an initial vowel. Occasionally, Chinese ideographs are interspersed. An older way of writing from top to bottom and right
to left, in imitation of the Chinese, has given way to the "western" direction in horizontal lines.

9.3. Burushaski

Burushaski is spoken by about 20,000 people in the Karakoram
Mountains in the western part of Pakistan's Kashmir. Although
the sound system shows analogies to Indic and the grammar to
Dravidian languages, no relationship has been established, and
the language seems to be completely isolated. The declension
and conjugation are complicated, and four classes of nouns are
distinguished, one for men, one for women, a third for other
living beings, fruits, and manufactured articles, and a fourth
for other objects and abstract concepts. Syntactical relation is
obtained largely by prefixes and suffixes. The language has
never been reduced to writing.

9.4. Paleo-Siberian Languages

Six languages, spoken by a total population of about 20,000 in
the extreme northeast corner of Siberia, are remnants of a
Paleo-Siberian family that earlier extended over a much larger
part of northern Asia. The main language is *Chukchee* (self-

designation *luoravetlan)*, spoken by 11,000 persons in the part
of Siberia closest to Alaska. An enclave of a Paleo-Siberian
language with fewer than a thousand speakers is located as far
west as the Yenisei River. Writings use the Cyrillic alphabet.

9.5. Ainu

Ainu is a moribund language whose number of speakers has
constantly dwindled since the Ainu people battled with the
Japanese for possession of the islands, beginning in the eighth
century. Defeats, epidemics, assimilation have reduced the Ainu
to probably no more than 10,000 people. They are located on
the coast of Japan's northernmost island, Hokkaido, and in
southern Sakhalin in the USSR. This latter group is so small
that no separate count was taken in the 1959 Russian census.

While a racial relationship to Finns or Lapps has been suggested, no linguistic kinship can be established between Ainu
and any other tongue. It may well be the offspring of the ancestral language of the Japanese islands. The word *ainu* means
"human being." Ainu is agglutinative, using suffixes and enclitics. Syllables are generally open; long vowels are rare. Aside
from Bible translations, using Roman letters, there is no written literature.

9.6. Andamanese

Indigenes of the Andaman Islands in the Bay of Bengal, who
speak *Andamanese* in a number of tribal variants, have been
decimated in the last one hundred years and may now amount
to no more than 400. No kinship with any other tongue has
ever been found. The language is agglutinative. Prefixes serve
as classifiers, and there are three classes, used for humans, other
living creatures, and inanimate objects respectively. Suffixes
and postpositions denote syntactical relationships. There is no
inflection.

10. AFRICAN AND KHOIN LANGUAGES

Of the total 280 million inhabitants of Africa, about 160 million speak native Negro languages. Their territory extends from the Semito-Hamitic belt south of the Sahara and west of the Nile down to the very tip of the continent. Exemption must be made of the Khoin family, the speakers of English and Afrikaans in the Republic of South Africa, several Indian speech communities, and the superimposed European languages, notably French, English, and Portuguese. These are used commercially and administratively and have official or co-official status in over twenty-five countries that have gained their independence since 1945. Changes in Africa's political organization may speed research on the native languages, most of which are still unwritten. Oddly enough, the word *African* does not stem from any African language, but derives from the Latin word *aprica*, "sunny."

10.1. African Language Family

The great linguistic diversity characteristic of the tropical and subtropical regions in the Western Hemisphere and in the Pacific manifests itself also in Africa. An estimated total of seven hundred languages includes over fifty with more than 500,000 speakers each. Progress has been made toward valid classification of all African tongues, but their affinity and subgrouping are still uncertain. Although considered by some scholars an oversimplification, a convenient division is into a northern and a southern branch, separated approximately at the equator. The northern, Sudanic, branch includes about four hundred fifty languages, representing 90 million speakers; as many as sixteen groups have been differentiated. The southern branch, Bantu, comprises about two hundred fifty languages with as many as fourteen groups and 70 million speakers. A high degree of homogeneity is apparent so that the former existence of one common prototype of all African Negro languages may be posited.

SUDANIC BRANCH

The Sudanic branch has taken its name from the Arabic word for *black*, first applied to Moslem Negro tribes. At least fourteen languages of this branch are noteworthy because of regional importance, use as lingua franca, or number of speakers. *Fula* is spoken by 6 million people, with the largest concentrations in Nigeria and Guinea, but with scattered enclaves extending north and west as far as Dakar. *Mandingo,* with several dialects including Maninka, Bambara, and Dyula, is spoken by 4 million in Mali, Ivory Coast, Guinea, and neighboring states. *Mossi* (self-designation *mole*) with 3 million, is the main language of Upper Volta. It has 400,000 speakers in Mali. *Kpelle* is spoken by 700,000 in Liberia and Guinea. *Twi-Fante,* including Akan and Ashanti dialects, is spoken by 4 million in Ghana. *Mende* has over 1 million speakers in Sierra Leone. *Fon,* with 800,000 speakers, is the main language of Dahomey. *Ewe* is spoken by 1 million people in the coastal area of Togo and its neighbor Dahomey, but serves also as a lingua franca in adjoining regions.

Nigeria, with the largest population in Africa, also has more languages than any other nation, estimates running from sixty to two hundred fifty. *Hausa,* until recently considered a Sudanic language, but now found to be more akin to the Semito-

Hamitic family, is native to 7 million in the northern area and serves as the lingua franca over a wide territory. Of the Sudanic tongues in Nigeria, mention should be made of *Kanuri,* spoken by 2 million in the northeast and also in Chad and Niger; *Yoruba* in the southwest and *Ibo* in the southeast, each spoken by 5 million; *Bini* in between them with 500,000 speakers; and *Efik* with 1 million speakers in the southeast corner. The easternmost outpost of the Sudanic branch, *Nubian* is spoken by 1 million people in southern Sudan.

BANTU BRANCH

The word *Bantu* was originally applied to tribes in whose languages the word for "man" was similar, its root being *ntu.* The prefix *ba* is the plural designation of words for living beings so that *bantu* simply means "men." The assumption is that the Bantus spread southward from central Africa. In its national anthem, the Central African Republic calls itself the "Bantus' cradle" although the country is situated north of the linguistic borderline.

Kongo (self-designation *kiKongo; kong* meaning mountains) is spoken by over 1 million people in the two Congo republics. *Luba* has 3 million speakers in Katanga. *Lingala* is the native language of 700,000 people at the northern bend of the Congo River, but extends as an administrative and police language along a considerable length up and down the river. On the west coast, *Fang-Bulu* is spoken by 2 million people in southern Cameroun and neighboring Gabon. *Mbundu* has 2 million and *Ndongo* (self-designation *kiNdongo*) 1 million speakers in Angola.

On the east coast, *Swahili* (self-designation *kiSwaheli*) constitutes the most important idiom of all African languages. It was developed by Arab slave traders, but is now native to 11 million people, distributed over Tanganyika (5½ million), Kenya (2½ million), the Congo (2 million), Burundi (500,000),

with another 700,000 in Uganda, Zanzibar, and neighboring
islands. It is used as a lingua franca by additional millions
through Kenya, the Congo, and Tanganyika, where it may be
made official. In 1962, Swahili was proposed as Kenya's official
language, but lost out to English. The language has several
dialects, the speech of Zanzibar being considered the standard.
While its grammar is Bantu, the vocabulary has many Arabic
roots. The designation *Swahili* is derived from an Arabic word
meaning "coasts." The name of Africa's highest mountain, Kili-
manjaro, is Swahili for "mountain of spirits." There exists a
considerable literature, and several dozen newspapers are published in the language.

Kikuyu has over 1 million speakers in central Kenya, *Nyam-
wesi-Sukuma* over 1 million in the interior of Tanganyika.
Ganda is spoken by almost 2 million in Uganda, where it is
co-official with English, *Ruanda* (self-designation *kiNyaRu-
anda*) by 5 million, divided equally between Rwanda and
the Congo, and *Rundi* (self-designation *kiRundi*) by 2 million
in the Congo and Burundi. *Makua* with 1½ million and
Thonga with over 1 million speakers are native to Mozambique. *Shona* has 2 million speakers, mostly in Southern Rhodesia. *Nyanja* is spoken by 1 million people in Nyasaland and
by 300,000 in Northern Rhodesia, where *Bemba*, native to
900,000, represents the largest linguistic group and is gaining
in stature by use as a lingua franca.

The Republic of South Africa has speakers of nine major
Bantu languages, including *Sotho* (self-designation *seSotho*)
and *Zulu* with 3½ million speakers each, *Xhosa* with 2 million, the latter two closely related to each other, and *Tswana*,
of Sotho affinity, with 1 million, reaching into Southern Rhodesia and Bechuanaland. SiNdebele is a Zulu dialect spoken
mainly in Southern Rhodesia.

African languages make abundant use of prefixes, suffixes,
and infixes. Prefixes show number and other grammatical relationships of nouns; Zulu *umu* indicates the singular and
aba the plural. With the aid of prefixes, nouns are divided into

as many as twenty classes. All modifiers and other words in a
sentence with a syntactical relation to a noun show this connection by a concord of either identical or alliterative prefixes. This brings about a sonorous intonation, and the effect
is heightened by generally open syllables. Consonantal clusters
are rare. Words borrowed from foreign tongues reflect this so
that *Christ* becomes *Kiristi*.

Especially in the northern Bantu languages and even more
in some Sudanic tongues, musical pitch serves the purpose of
semantic or grammatical distinctions, notably in the verbal
system. Thus, a low tone expresses a positive statement, a
plural, or the person addressed, while a high tone indicates
negation, a singular, or the speaker. Similar tonal differences
signify the object function of a noun. The absence of grammatical inflections results in rigid syntax.

Sudanic languages usually show the plural of nouns by suffixes. Diphthongs are rare, nasal sounds abound. An inclusive
and exclusive first person plural pronoun is found in some
western Sudanic languages.

Aside from Bible translations, only a limited number of
African languages has ever been reduced to writing. Literacy
in Africa seldom exceeds five to ten percent of the adult native population. Swahili was the first African language to be
written before the Europeans arrived. Fula, Kanuri, and Nubian use Arabic letters; other writings are in a modified
Roman alphabet. The uniform standard proposed by the International African Institute in London includes symbols of
the International Phonetic Alphabet and has gained wide
acceptance, notably in Nigeria.

10.2. Khoin Family

The Khoin language family includes *Hottentot* (self-designation *nama), Bushman* (self-designation *san),* and three minor
idioms in Tanganyika. The Boers coined the term *Hottentot*

in derision of its speech sounds. It is spoken in South-West Africa by fewer than 200,000 people. Bushman has only 50,000 speakers in South-West Africa with very small groups in Bechuanaland. It is believed that at one time the Khoin people occupied a much larger area in southern and eastern Africa.

Words are predominantly monosyllabic, but disyllables exist. Pronouns have a first person inclusive and exclusive plural form and a dual. Phonetically peculiar are the clicks, produced by opening the lips, inhaling, and withdrawing the tongue from contact with the roof of the mouth or the teeth against which it was pressed, resulting in a sucking sound. According to the place of articulation, four clicks are distinguished which with the combination of consonants may form as many as twenty-four phonemes. Some have spread to such neighboring southern Bantu languages, as Zulu, Sotho, and Xhosa. The latter has three clicks, and the spelling of its name reflects an aspirated click.

11. MALAYO - POLYNESIAN LANGUAGES

The area covered by the Malayo-Polynesian group is far more extended than that of any other family; it stretches more than half around the globe, from Madagascar to Easter Island, with Hawaii as the northernmost and New Zealand the southernmost apex. Australia and the interior of New Guinea are not included. It is believed that the people of this territory wandered west and east from a homeland located near present Malaya, and successively occupied the outlying districts, arriving at Hawaii, for instance, between A.D. 700 and 900. This spread may have begun early; its start may even antedate the division of Indo-European languages, assumed to have begun in the fourth or third millennium B.C.

The thousands of islands and the lack of communication in former times favored the development of dialectical variations, many of which later turned into individual languages. Only the more important tongues have been studied sufficiently to permit some grouping, and a comprehensive classification cannot yet be attempted. There are probably as many as five hundred languages, spoken by an aggregate of 130 million persons. A separation, geographic and presumably genetic, may be made into the Western Malayo-Polynesian idioms spoken in Madagascar, the Malay Peninsula, Taiwan, the Philippines, Borneo, and Indonesia, and the Eastern Malayo-Polynesian comprising New Zealand and the Pacific islands. The latter branch includes the Melanesian, Micronesian, and Polynesian groups and has many more individual languages than the western. The insular languages have comparatively few speakers and their total amounts to only 1 million.

11.1. Western Branch

Culturally and commercially, the western branch is the more important of the two. Spatially isolated by the Indian Ocean, Madagascar, the size of France, has about 5 million speakers of *Malagasy*. In Southeast Asia, *Malay* is the most important language, not for its number of native speakers, which is only 17 million, but for the fact that it has long been used in a pidginized form, known as Bazaar Malay, as the lingua franca in coastal regions from Sumatra to the Philippines. Those to whom Malay is the mother tongue are located principally in Malaya, on Borneo, and on the northeastern coast of Sumatra. In 1945, a version of Malay differing from the Malay proper mostly in its vocabulary and phraseology, and based on Bazaar Malay was promulgated as the national and only official language of Indonesia. This form of Malay is named *Indonesian* (self-designation *bahasa Indonesia, bahasa* meaning "language") and is the result of planned development during two decades. The patriotic fervor with which the youth of a country exceeding the 100-million population mark, hailed the use of this tongue as a unifying force and forswore all others may justify the prediction that in the near future there will be considerably more than the present 12 million native speakers of Indonesian, that this idiom may drift away from the Malay in the north and eventually become a separate language.

There are said to be two hundred languages and dialects throughout Indonesia, the world's most scattered country. *Javanese,* spoken by 45 million people in the northern and eastern parts of Java, boasts a rich literature going back to the eighth century. On the same island, in the southwest and around the capital of Djakarta, 14 million speak *Sundanese. Madurese* is spoken by 7 million people on Madura, and *Balinese* by 2 mil-

lion on Bali. Another 2 million speak *Batak* in the interior
of northern Sumatra. *Bugi* is spoken by 2 million on Celebes,
and *Dayak* by over 1 million in the interior of Kalimantan
(the southern part of Borneo) and Sarawak.

On Taiwan, a few thousand people in the interior speak
languages of this branch, and there are a number of related
languages in the Philippines; among the more widely spoken
are *Visayan*, spoken by 11 million people on the central
islands; *Tagalog*, the official language, spoken by 6 million,
primarily in central Luzon; *Ilocano* (self-designation *iloko*),
spoken by 3 million in northern Luzon; and *Bikol*, spoken
by 2 million in southern Luzon.

11.2. Eastern Branch

A multitude of Melanesian and Polynesian languages is located east of an arc drawn from the Palau and Mariana islands
to New Zealand, including the southeastern coastal strip of
Papua. The greatest diversity occurs in the Bismarck Archipel-
ago and on the Solomons. Outside this area, the following are
of interest: *Fiji*, spoken on the Fiji Islands by 100,000 people;
Samoan, spoken in Western and American Samoa by 100,000;
Maori, spoken in the interior of New Zealand by 75,000 descendants of its original inhabitants; *Tongan*, spoken by 70,000
on Tonga; *Chamorro* by 30,000 on Guam; *Tahitian*, by 30,000
on Tahiti; *Hawaiian*, by 25,000; *Ponapese* and *Yapese*, spoken
by 10,000 and 7,000 respectively on Ponape, Yap, and nearby
islands in the Carolines. So-called "Neo-Melanesian" is not
of this family, but a kind of Pidgin English.

These Malayo-Polynesian languages are characterized by a
profusion of vowels and fullness of vowel sounds, a corresponding dearth of consonants and the avoidance of heaping of consonants. Polynesian tongues especially tend to have fewer consonants and generally open syllables. Roots are preferably di-

syllabic. In a sentence, words follow each other without grammatical connection, which has to be deduced, as in Malay
orang utan, "man forest," *mata hari*, "eye day," meaning sun.
Derivatives are also formed by affixes and infixes. Those languages that have an alphabet generally use Roman letters with
some modifications. Javanese and Madurese, however, may
still employ the Javanese alphabet, derived from the southern
Indian variation of Devanagari. Malay has changed its alphabet twice and now uses Roman letters. Tagalog uses three
accents and the tilde over *ng*, which is considered one letter
and stands for the velar nasal. The unique hieroglyphics on
the pagan Rongo-rongo boards found on Easter Island constitute the only known native writing in Polynesia. They have
not yet been fully deciphered.

11.3. Hawaiian

Hawaiian is the indigenous language of the Hawaiian Islands,
nicknamed the *Aloha State*, from the greeting *aloha*, meaning
"hello" or "good-by." The language is considered one of the
most musical in the world; it has only fifteen distinct sounds.
It was reduced to writing by missionaries in the 1820's. Hawaiian place names are approximations of the original melodious
sounds as heard by the first visitors. The British sea captain
James Cook, who discovered the islands in 1778 and called
them Sandwich Islands, spelled the name of the largest island
Owhyhee.

The alphabet consists of twelve letters, five vowels and seven
consonants. Each letter is sounded. The stress is generally on
the penultimate and on alternating preceding syllables. The
vowels are pronounced as in Italian, *a* as in 'lark,' *e* as in
'they,' *i* as in 'marine,' *o* as in 'lone,' and *u* as in 'rule.' Diphthongization takes place in the case of *ai*, pronounced as in
'aisle,' or *au*, pronounced as in 'lounge.' The consonants are
h, k, l, m, n, p, w, the last usually vocalic, but consonantal

before a final letter. There is also a glottal stop, called *uina* in Hawaiian, and sometimes written as an apostrophe as in *'ae*, "yes." In adapting English names, letters not in the Hawaiian alphabet are occasionally taken over, but more commonly a replacement takes place, in the liquids, *r* becoming *l*. Examples are *Lukela*, "Luther," *Lopaka* "Robert," *Malia* 'Mary.' The same process applies to imported foreign phrases, like *Mele Kalikimaka*, "Merry Christmas." Different inclusive and exclusive personal and possessive pronouns exist for the first person plural.

Hawaiian is now the mother tongue of a mere fraction of the inhabitants of the Islands. Native speakers are variously estimated to number between 10,000 and 50,000, and they are usually bilingual. Only 21 percent of the state's population of 600,000 are of Hawaiian or partly Hawaiian blood, for there has been heavy intermarriage with other groups, most of whom, like the Japanese, belong to other language families. On one island, Niihau, a few hundred people are kept out of contact with the outside world and are considered the only remaining group of pure Hawaiians. On the outer islands, the language has become increasingly pidginized through the influence of English and other western tongues. Aside from courses offered by the University of Hawaii, the language is not taught in the state, and where an interest in it is kept alive, it is often with the intent of providing a tourist attraction.

12. PAPUAN AND AUSTRALIAN LANGUAGES

The island of New Guinea constitutes linguistically the greatest unknown quantity. This second largest island of the world has an area equal to France and West Germany combined and its population is estimated to exceed two million, but its interior remains isolated and largely unexplored. The western part is now incorporated into Indonesia; the eastern sections are administered by Australia.

Resulting mainly from the peoples' isolation in practically impenetrable jungles and mountain lands and from their animosity toward each other, there arose a large number of languages, possibly one hundred and fifty, some spoken by as few as fifty people. *Bentoeni* with about 100,000 speakers in the western part of New Guinea may be the most widely spoken language. Until these tribes can be fully studied, the extent and kinship of their tongues remain largely a matter of conjecture. In the absence of precise data, the number of languages has been variously estimated to be between one hundred and six hundred with the bulk in the section of Papua proper. This Australian territory on the southeastern part of the island has lent its name also to the entire island and the term Papuan to the aggregate of languages spoken on it and in the surrounding area, which is of necessity a geographic rather than genetic way of classification.

Some written form exists for sixty-five languages and dialects, mostly in the nature of partial Bible translations. Missionaries are aware of the great need of reaching the other peoples, and the 1959 issue of the *Ethnologue,* published by the Wycliffe Bible Translators as a compilation of languages that still lack the Bible and therefore any written form, lists a total of 767 tribes in this area. Without a doubt, many of these speak idioms that are mere dialectical variations, yet the separation into extremely small groups which has existed for centuries is bound to have resulted in many tongues that are no longer mutually intelligible. One of these, *Ono,* spoken by about 4,000 people on the northeastern coast of the island, shows infixion and great variation in the verbal system, but the nouns lack declension and gender. Some languages have inclusive and exclusive first person plural pronouns. No affinity is traceable to Polynesian tongues or those of other families.

The aboriginal languages of Australia are believed to total about one hundred, with an ever-decreasing number of speakers, probably not more than 200,000. A valid classification of these languages is not yet available but there seem to be at least five groups, of which the most interesting is the one located in the extreme north in Arnhem Land and adjoining districts. In this group, a distinction may be made by the number of classes into which nouns are divided, from two to nine. It is somewhat incongruous to find among Australian languages some so primitive that they have no words for numerals beyond three and some with such a linguistic distinction as separate dual and trial forms of pronominal number, as in *Worora,* spoken by 1,000 people in the northwest.

If in spite of meager evidence a general judgment can be made on native Australian languages, it may be said that consonantal clusters are frequent, that the grammar is inflecting, that numerals are scanty, and that meaningful gestures are used as semantic reinforcement to a considerable extent, especially in intertribal communication. There is no written form of these languages, and the inroads of civilization doom the remaining aboriginal tongues to early extinction. The fate of the dead Tasmanian languages is a sad parallel experience.

13. AMERINDIAN LANGUAGES

It is believed that at the time the Europeans arrived there, the Western Hemisphere was inhabited by about 40 million people who may have spoken as many as eighteen hundred different languages. Few of these have maintained or surpassed their original number of speakers, and almost two-thirds have become extinct. Under the impact of the superimposed colonial languages, English, Spanish, Portuguese, French, and Dutch, the number of native speakers of Amerindian languages has dwindled to 12 million.

Most of these reside in South and Central America. In Guatemala, Indian speakers are in the majority with 60 percent of the population using twenty languages. In Peru 53 percent and in Bolivia and Paraguay about half of the population speak an Indian language, but speakers of Indian tongues are minorities in the other Latin American countries. In the United States, only about 250,000 speakers of Indian remain. However, they represent up to two hundred languages. Throughout the hemisphere, the great diversity of languages is striking; it may be explained by low population density and the virtual inaccessibility of tropical and mountainous regions, as well as by the tremendous area involved. Estimates of Latin American indigenous languages range from four hundred to thirteen hundred; a precise number is unavailable as long as large territories are still unexplored. As many as one hundred different families have been proposed. Considering the demise of many isolated speech communities, it seems reasonable to posit two hundred North American languages with 2 million speakers and five hundred Latin American languages with 10 million speakers.

13.1. North American Branch

The indigenous languages of North America have been classified on the basis of structural resemblance, and six large groupings are differentiated. The Eskimo-Aleut extends from eastern Siberia to Greenland, running mostly north of the Arctic Circle, but including almost the entire coast of Alaska. The 50,000 speakers of *Eskimo* (self-designation *inuit*) represent the main language of this group of 60,000. Over half of them now live in Greenland, where they have their own newspaper and radio station; other groups are in Alaska, Canada, and Siberia. The Canadian magazine *Inuktitut,* "the Eskimo Way," is printed in the syllabic script devised by nineteenth-century Anglican missionaries. It consists of twelve symbols convertible into forty-eight by shifts of position. Western Eskimos are familiar with the Roman characters. Some scholars connect the Eskimo-Aleut group with Altaic, Paleo-Siberian, or even Sino-Tibetan languages.

The Athabascan group of about 100,000 speakers occupies the interior of Alaska and northwestern Canada. When combined with three other languages whose kinship is uncertain, it is also called Na-Dene. Migration between A.D. 1000 and 1500 created a southern enclave extending through eastern Arizona, New Mexico, and southwest Texas. To this section belongs the most viable North American Indian language, *Navaho,* spoken by about 80,000 people in New Mexico and Arizona. *Apache* dialects are spoken by about 5,000 in a wide area extending southeast from the Navaho territory into Texas and Mexico. The Algonquian group of 80,000 speakers covers the largest territory of all, running from Vancouver Island through Canada to Newfoundland and down the Atlantic coast to North Carolina. Its most enduring language is *Ojibwa,* spoken by 40,000 in the Great Lakes region. *Penutian* and related dialects are spoken by 20,000 people in Oregon and northern California. The Hoka-Siouan group of 70,000 speakers includes a Siouan branch in the Central Great Plains west of the Mississippi, and an Iroquoian branch in the south of the St. Lawrence River valley. The appellation *Iroquois* is a nickname coined by the French because the Indians frequently used the words *hiro,* "I have spoken," and *koué,* "with joy" or "with sorrow," to finish their speeches. The southeastern United States is also Hoka-Siouan speech territory, and here *Cherokee* is still spoken by 40,000 people in the North Carolina mountains. This was the first North American Indian language to be written. The invention of the Cherokee alphabet in 1821 was the achievement of an unschooled tribal chieftain, Sequoyah, who fashioned eighty-six phonetic symbols. After initial ridicule and vicissitudes, he became the hero of his people and was honored by having the world's tallest tree named after him.

The Uto-Aztecan group of 1 million speakers extends from Nevada and Utah into Mexico. *Nahuatl,* now spoken by over 800,000 people, mainly in Mexico, is the modern offspring of *Aztec,* the language of the ancient Aztec civilization; its speakers may have numbered 5 million before the Spanish conquest and extended as far south as Panama. The typical Aztec *tl* phoneme is reduced to *l* or *t* in certain sections, resulting in dialects named Nahual and Nahuat respectively.

13.2. Latin American Branch

While considerable progress has been made in classifying North American languages, the picture in Central and South America is still greatly blurred. Most outstanding of all Amerindian languages is *Quechua,* spoken in several dialects by 6 million people in Peru, Bolivia, Ecuador, Brazil, and Argen-

tina. This was the administrative language of the Inca empire.
As a way of writing, the ancient Peruvians used the *quipu,* a
combination of knotted cords that conveyed a message by their
shape and color. Quechua, now taught along with Spanish in
Peruvian schools, is probably one of the few indigenous tongues
that has gained in numbers of speakers since the advent of the
Spaniards. Its growth is partly at the expense of *Aymara,* which
is still spoken in Peru and Bolivia by over 1 million people.
Guarani, spoken by over 1 million people, is native to Paraguay and Brazil. *Arawak* and *Carib,* each spoken over a wide
area by about 200,000 in a large number of dialectical variations, have had an odd linguistic history. When the Caribs
conquered the Arawakan tribes in the fourteenth century, they
killed the men and married the women. The wives continued
to speak their Arawak idiom, while their husbands spoke Carib;
children were brought up bilingual, but when they became
adults, the men continued to speak Carib and the women
Arawak, a division that persists in some areas. Today, Arawak
speech is heard in Venezuela, the Guianas, and the Greater
Antilles, while Carib is spoken in the Lesser Antilles and in
the territory between the Orinoco and Amazon rivers.

In Central America, *Maya,* the language of the Mayan empire, survives in a number of variations in the speech of 1¼
million people in Yucatan, Guatemala, Honduras, and British
Honduras. Mayans are believed to have been the first inhabitants of America, having migrated across the Bering Sea from
Asia to Alaska and thence southward. The Mayans, who ex-
celled in astronomy and mathematics, had created a system of
writing in pre-Columbian time; inscriptions exist on build-
ings, and three codices are preserved in Dresden, Paris, and
Madrid. The writing material was created from the pulp of the
Agave americana, the maguey plant, which served the Mexi-
cans as the papyrus did the Egyptians. Mayan writing consists of about 2500 hieroglyphs, with the human head the most
frequently encountered symbol. Only parts of this writing
have been deciphered.

American Indian languages have widely differing characteristics both in phonemes and in morphology. A feature common
to many is polysyntheticism, resulting in long words that constitute phrases, with a corresponding lack of inflections. This
may be an indication that most of these languages share one
common ancestor. The polysynthetic structure may be illustrated by Eskimo *nagligivara,* "I love him," *nagligetyangelagit,*
"I do not love you," *nagligelautyangelagit,* "did I love you?"
nagligeungnangegupko, "if I am not able to love him." None
of these parts would convey any definite meaning if used by
itself. On the other hand, Maya and related languages, thought
to be older, are not synthetic but have mostly monosyllabic
roots. Indian geographical names often show polysynthesis.
Massachusetts means "big hill people," *Omaha,* "upstream people," *Mississippi,* "big river," *Missouri,* "canoe river." Amerindian languages, especially Cherokee, Apache, and Navaho,
have been used in times of war to transmit uncoded messages
on the theory that these idioms would be unknown to the
enemy.

14. CONSTRUCTED LANGUAGES

The desirability of having one language as common medium of communication between all peoples of the world has been recognized for at least three centuries. The psychological barrier of national prejudice has so far prevented agreement on one particular natural language to be designated as the lingua franca and to be accepted by all nations as the means of inter-language communication. A solution may lie in the invention of an artificial tongue. Ideally its structure should not favor any existing language; it might be logically built and thus acquired with greater ease than a second natural language. Since the time that Descartes proposed such an invention in 1629, about five hundred artificial languages have been devised. Some of them have flourished for a short period, others have enjoyed considerable groups of advocates.

During the last one hundred years, the expansion of international contacts and the increasing speed and extent of means of transportation and communication have intensified interest in an international language. This agitation is buttressed by the lofty thought that mutual understanding would decrease the possibilities of wars, a theory that is unfortunately not borne out by the many armed conflicts that have occurred at different times between populations speaking the same language. Attempts have been made to construct a neutral idiom without relation to any existing tongue, but none of these has ever gained wide attention. Most artificial languages either simplify existing languages, like *Basic English,* or blend elements from a number of them, favoring especially the Indo-

European tongues. The first such endeavor was the creation of *Volapük,* meaning "world speech," by the German priest Johann Martin Schleyer in 1879; it at one time claimed 200,000 speakers.

14.1 Esperanto

The most successful constructed language has been *Esperanto,* meaning "hopeful." It has survived two major attempts at reform since its invention in 1887 by the oculist Ludwik L. Zamenhof, who lived in Bialystok, a border town where Polish, Russian, Lithuanian, German, and Yiddish were spoken. Esperanto is the only artificial language that has a world-wide body of speakers; its press publishes over a hundred periodicals. More than 8,000 books have been published in Esperanto, and it is taught in about 600 schools. The estimates of the number of speakers, identifiable by a five-pointed green star in the lapel or on a button, vary but may reach 5 million, scattered over more than eighty countries. They are located especially in the small nations, but the largest group in the Western Hemisphere is in Brazil.

Esperanto is chiefly a Romance-Germanic blend constructed from elements of occidental tongues and with an agglutinative grammatical structure. The alphabet consists of twenty-eight Roman letters, which are always pronounced and never change their sound values. Additional symbols are created by adding the circumflex to *c, g, h, j, s,* to reflect the sounds as in 'leech,' 'liege,' 'loch,' 'leisure,' and 'leash.' A breve over the *u* indicates a sound similar to the English *w.* A vowel ending designates the part of speech or verbal form; thus, adjectives end in *a,* adverbs in *e,* infinitives in *i,* nouns in *o,* imperatives in *u.* The present tense ends in *as,* the past in *is,* the future in *os,* conditional in *us;* active participles end in *anta, inta, onta,* passive in *ata, ita, ota.* Nouns and adjectives form the plural by adding *j* and the accusative by adding *n.* There are no other inflectional endings.

The word roots, taken from various European languages, may be combined with ten prefixes and twenty-seven suffixes so that as many as fifty derivatives may result from one root. This gives the language great flexibility and possibility of ex-pansion, though it keeps the basic word stock within the limit of 3500 and eliminates the necessity of memorizing many ad-ditional concepts for which other languages usually have in-dividual roots. An example is the extension of the root *patr,* which becomes *patro,* "father," *patra,* "fatherly," *patroj,* "fathers," *patrino,* "mother," *patrinoj,* "mothers," *gepatroj,* "parents," *bopatro,* "father-in-law," and so on.

14.2. *Interlingua*

Another constructed language that enjoys a considerable following is *Interlingua.* An early forerunner of this system was Giuseppe Peano's *Latino sine flexione,* developed in 1903. It was followed in 1922 by Edgar de Wahl's *Occidental,* later renamed *Interlingua.* The present Interlingua was finally pre-sented in 1948, the end result of painstaking scholarship of a team of experts who had begun their task in 1924.

The 27,000 words of Interlingua represent a "pan-Occi-dental" form extracted by comparison of roots and derivatives in eight source languages, five Romance: Latin, Italian, Span-ish, Portuguese, French; and three others, English, German, Russian, reflecting the basic homogeneity of the western lan-guages. The grammar, primarily Romance, is analytic and stripped to the barest essentials. As in the establishment of the vocabulary, there is one basic rule: no feature is included if it is missing in one of the source languages. Thus verbs have no change of stem and no inflection within the tense; nouns have no gender and no inflection except the plural *s.* Only standard Roman letters are used, with "classical" pro-nunciation and without diacritical marks.

Since Interlingua draws heavily on the living Romance languages and Latin and since the scientific vocabulary of all western languages is steeped with words from this source, Interlingua is especially useful for international contacts of scientists who find it easy to recognize the words from the similarity, if not complete likeness, to their own tongues. Several international congresses have used Interlingua, two monthlies are printed in the language, and Interlingua abstracts are published in some twenty scientific and technical journals.

A comparison of the identical text in Esperanto and Interlingua may demonstrate their respective features: a) *La vagonaro iris tra la bela vilaĝo. En la strato mi vidis multe da geknaboj kiuj iris al lernejo kun siaj libroj. Ili studas geografion, historion, kaj fremdajn lingvojn.* b) *Le traino passava per le belle village. In le strata io videva multe garsones e pueras qui vadeva al schola con lor libros. Illes stude geographia, historia, e linguas estranie.*

APPENDIX A

Genetic Classification of Principal Living Languages

All 207 languages discussed in the text are included here. Families are listed under the continents where the ancestral language arose even though the languages may now be more conspicuous in other regions. Within each continent and subgrouping, the order is by number of native speakers. Terms in parentheses are self-designations, where different. For every language, the country with the largest number of speakers is given. A second country is listed if mention seems warranted by a relatively large concentration of that language's speakers. No implication should be drawn that there may not be additional countries with sizable numbers of speakers; for such information the reader is referred to the text.

EUROPE

I. INDO-EUROPEAN (*about 140 languages*) . 1,580 million

  A. WESTERN . . . . 830 million

    1. *GERMANIC* . . . . 420 million

      a. *Western* . . . . 400 million

        English . . . . 265 million USA, UK

        German (*deutsch*) . . . 100 million Germany, Austria

Dutch-Flemish . . . . 17 million Netherlands,
(*nederlands-vlaams*)   Belgium

Yiddish (*yidish*) . . . . 4 million USA (N.Y.),
                                                   Israel

Afrikaans . . . . . . 3 million South Africa

Frisian (*friesisch*) . . . 300,000 Netherlands

Luxemburgian . . . 300,000 Luxemburg
(*lezebuurjesh*)

b. *Northern* . . . . 20 million

Swedish (*svensk*) . . . . 9 million Sweden,
                                                   USA

Danish (*dansk*) . . . . 5 million Denmark

Norwegian (*norsk*) . . . 4 million Norway,
                                                   USA

Icelandic (*íslenzka*) . . . 160,000 Iceland,
                                                   Faroe Isl'ds

2. *ROMANCE* . . . . 390 million

a. *Eastern* . . . . 80 million

Italian (*italiano*) . . . . 55 million Italy

Rumanian (*românește*) . 20 million Rumania
                                                   USSR
                                                   (Mold. SSR)

Sardinian (*sardu*) . . . 1 million Italy
                                                   (Sardinia)

Rhaeto-Romanic . . . . 600,000 Italy,
                                                   Switzerland

Latin . . . . (liturgical)

b. *Western* . . . . 310 million

Spanish (*español*) . . . 145 million Mexico,
                                                   Spain

Portuguese (*português*) . . 85 million Brazil,
                                             Portugal

French (*français*) . . . . 65 million France,
                                             Canada

Catalan . . . . 5 million Spain

French Creole . . . . 5 million Haiti
(*français-créole*)

Papiamento . . . . . 200,000 Netherlands
                                             Antilles

Portuguese Creole . . . 200,000 Cape Verde
                                             Islands

Ladino . . . . 140,000 Turkey,
                                             Greece

3. *CELTIC* . . . . 3 million

  a. *Goidelic* . . . . 1 million

    Gaelic (*gaeilge*) . . . . 1 million Ireland

    Scottish Gaelic (*gaelig*) . . 100,000 UK
                                           (Scotland)

  b. *Brythonic* . . . . 2 million

    Breton (*breiz*) . . . . . 1 million France

    Welsh (*cymraeg*) . . . . 1 million UK (Wales),
                                           USA

4. *GREEK* (*ellinika*) . . . . 10 million Greece

B. Eastern . . . . 750 million

1. *BALTO-SLAVIC* . . . . 270 million

  a. *Baltic* . . . . 5 million

    Lithuanian (*lietuviškai*) 3 million USSR (Lithu-
                                           anian SSR)

Latvian (*latviski*) . . . .   1 million USSR (Lat-
                                          vian SSR)

b. *Slavic* . . . . 260 million

Eastern . . . . 180 million

Russian (*russki*) . . . . 135 million USSR

Ukrainian (*ukraïnski*) . .   38 million USSR
                                          (Ukrainian
                                          SSR)

Byelorussian . . . .   7 million USSR
(*bielorusski*)   (Byelorus-
                                          sian SSR)

Western . . . . 50 million

Polish (*polski*) . . . . .   33 million Poland,
                                          USA

Czech (*česky*) . . . . .   10 million Czechoslo-
                                          vakia

Slovak (*slovensky*) . . .   4 million Czechoslo-
                                          vakia

Lusatian (*serbski*) . . .   100,000 Germany

Southern . . . . 25 million

Serbo-Croatian . . . .   15 million Yugoslavia
(*srp, hrvat*)

Bulgarian (*bulgarski*) . .   7 million Bulgaria

Slovenian (*slovenski*) . .   2 million Yugoslavia

Macedonian . . . . .   1 million Yugoslavia
(*makedonski*)

Old Church Slavic . . . . (liturgical)

2. *ALBANIAN* (*shqip*) . . .   3 million Albania,
                                          Yugoslavia

3. *ARMENIAN* (*hayeren*) . . 4 million USSR
                                      (Armenian
                                      SSR)

4. *INDO-IRANIAN* (*about 100 languages*) . 470 million

  a. *Indic* . . . . 430 million

    Hindi-Urdu . . . . 185 million India (N),
                                      Pakistan

    Bengali . . . . 85 million Pakistan,
                                      India (E)

    Punjabi . . . . 37 million Pakistan,
                                      India (NW)

    Marathi . . . . 35 million India (W)

    Gujarati . . . . 22 million India (W)

    Oriya . . . . 15 million India (E)

    Rajasthani . . . . . 15 million India (W)

    Nepali . . . . 8 million Nepal,
                                      India (N)

    Sinhalese . . . . . 8 million Ceylon

    Assamese . . . . . 6 million India (E)

    Sindhi . . . . 4 million Pakistan

    Kashmiri . . . . . 2 million India (W),
                                      Pakistan

    Bhili . . . . 1 million India (W)

    Romany . . . . . . 1 million Hungary,
                                      Spain

    Sanskrit . . . . (liturgical)

    Pali . . . . (liturgical)

  b. *Iranian* . . . . 40 million

    Persian (*farsi*) . . . . . 15 million Iran,
                                      Afghanistan

Pashto . . . . 14 million Afghanistan,
Pakistan

Kurdish . . . . 5 million Turkey,
Iran

Baluchi . . . . 1 million Pakistan

Tadzhik . . . . 1 million USSR (Tadzhik SSR)

Avestan . . . . (liturgical)

II. CAUCASIAN (*about 25 languages*) . . . . 5 million

A. NORTHERN (*about 20 languages*) . . . . 2 million

Chechen . . . . 400,000 USSR
(Checheno-
Ing. SSR)

Kabardin . . . . . 200,000 USSR
(Kabardin-
ian ASSR)

Circassian . . . . . 100,000 USSR
(Cherkess
ASSR)

Abkhaz . . . . 70,000 USSR
(Abkhazian
ASSR)

B. SOUTHERN (*4 languages*) . . . . 3 million

Georgian (*k'art'veli*) . . . 3 million USSR
(Georgian
SSR)

III. BASQUE (*euskara*) . . . 800,000 Spain,
France

ASIA

IV. SINO-TIBETAN (*about 30 languages*) . . . 760 million

   A. SINITIC . . . . 690 million

Chinese-Mandarin (*kuo yu*)	. . . 515 million	China (N)
Cantonese (*yueh*)	. . . . 55 million	China (Canton)
Wu	. . . . 55 million	China (Shanghai)
Fukienese (*min*)	. . . . 50 million	China (Fukien), Taiwan
Hakka	. . . . . . 20 million	China (Kwang-tung)

   B. TIBETO-BURMAN . . . . 70 million

Thai	. . . . 24 million	Thailand, China (Yunnan)
Burmese	. . . . . . 18 million	Burma
Tibetan	. . . . . . 7 million	China (Tibet)
Lolo (*nesu*)	. . . . . 3 million	China (Czechwan, Yunnan)
Miao	. . . . 3 million	China (Kweichow, Hunan)

Lao . . . .   2 million Laos

Shan . . . .   2 million Burma,
                                 China
                                 (Yunnan)

V. SEMITO-HAMITIC (*about 20 languages*) . . 125 million

A. SEMITIC . . . . 100 million

Arabic . . . . . . 90 million Egypt,
                              Morocco

Amharic . . . . . . 7 million Ethiopia

Hebrew (*ivrit*) . . . . . 1 million Israel

Tigrinya . . . . . .   500,000 Ethiopia

Aramaic-Syriac . . .   200,000 Turkey,
                                Iraq

Tigre . . . .   100,000 Ethiopia

South Arabic . . . .   50,000 Muscat and
                                Oman

Ethiopic (*ge'ez*) . . . . (liturgical)

B. HAMITIC . . . . 25 million

Hausa . . . . 9 million Nigeria,
                              Niger

Berber . . . . . . 6 million Morocco,
                             Algeria

Galla (*oromo*) . . . . 6 million Ethiopia
                                  Kenya

Somali . . . . . . 3 million Somalia,
                             Ethiopia

Coptic . . . . (liturgical)

VI. DRAVIDIAN (*about 10 languages*) . . . . 120 million

Telugu	42 million	India (S)
Tamil	37 million	India (S), Ceylon
Kanarese	17 million	India (S)
Malayalam	15 million	India (S)
Gondi	1 million	India (E)
Brahui	200,000	Pakistan

VII. JAPANESE (*nihongo*) . . . 95 million Japan

VIII. URALIC-ALTAIC (*about 40 languages*) . 90 million

A. URALIC . . . . 20 million

1. *FINNIC* . . . . 8 million

Finnish (*suomi*)	5 million	Finland
Estonian (*eesti*)	1 million	USSR (Estonian SSR)
Mordvin	1 million	USSR (Mordovian ASSR)
Lapp (*sâme*)	40,000	Norway, Sweden

2. *UGRIC* . . . . 12 million

Hungarian (*magyar*) . .	12 million	Hungary, Rumania

3. *SAMOYEDIC* 25,000

Samoyed (*nenets*) . . .	22,000	USSR (W Siberia)

B. ALTAIC . . . . 70 million

1. *TURKIC* . . . . 65 million

Turkish *(türkçe)* . . . . 27 million Turkey

Azerbaijani *(azeri)* . . . 7 million Iran, USSR
(Azerbaijan
SSR)

Uzbek . . . . 7 million USSR
(Uzbek SSR)

Kazakh . . . . 5 million USSR (Kazakh SSR),
China

Tatar . . . . 5 million USSR (Tatar ASSR)

Uighur . . . . 4 million China
(Sinkiang)

Chuvash . . . . 1 million USSR (Chuvash ASSR)

Kirgiz . . . . 1 million USSR (Kirgiz SSR)

Turkoman . . . . . 1 million USSR
(Turkmen
SSR)

2. *MONGOLIAN* . . . . 2 million

Khalkha . . . . . . 1 million Mongolia

3. *MANCHURIAN* 300,000

Manchu . . . . . 200,000 China
(Manchuria)

Tungus *(evenki)* . . . . 15,000 USSR
(E Siberia)

IX. SOUTHEAST ASIAN (*about 20 languages*) . 45 million

    A. VIETNAMESE . . . . . . 31 million Viet Nam

    B. MON-KHMER (*about 15 languages*) . . . . 8 million

        Cambodian (*khmer*) . . . 5 million Cambodia

        Mon . . . . 300,000 Burma

    C. MUNDA (*5 languages*) . . . . 5 million

        Santali . . . . . . 3 million India (E)

X. KOREAN (*chosenmal*) . . . 37 million Korea

XI. BURUSHASKI . . . . . 20,000 Pakistan

XII. PALEO-SIBERIAN (*6 languages*) 20,000

    Chukchee (*luoravetlan*) . 11,000 USSR

                               (NE Siberia)

XIII. AINU . . . . 10,000 Japan

XIV. ANDAMANESE . . . . . 400 India (Andaman Islands)

AFRICA

XV. AFRICAN (*about 700 languages*) . . . . 160 million

    A. SUDANIC (*about 450 languages*) . . . . . 90 million

        Fula . . . . 6 million Nigeria, Guinea

        Ibo . . . . 5 million Nigeria

Yoruba	5 million	Nigeria
Mandingo	4 million	Mali, Ivory Coast
Twi-Fante	4 million	Ghana
Mossi	3 million	Upper Volta, Mali
Kanuri	2 million	Nigeria, Chad
Efik	1 million	Nigeria
Ewe	1 million	Togo, Dahomey
Mende	1 million	Sierra Leone
Nubian	1 million	Sudan
Fon	800,000	Dahomey
Kpelle	700,000	Liberia, Guinea
Bini	500,000	Nigeria

B. BANTU (*about 250 languages*) . . . . . 70 million

Swahili (*kiSwaheli*) . . .	11 million	Tanganyika, Kenya
Ruanda (*kiNyaRuanda*) .	5 million	Rwanda, Congo (L.)
Sotho (*seSotho*)	4 million	South Africa
Zulu	4 million	South Africa
Luba	3 million	Congo (L.)
Fang-Bulu	2 million	Cameroun, Gabon
Ganda	2 million	Uganda

Makua	2 million	Mozambique
Mbundu	2 million	Angola
Rundi (*kiRundi*)	2 million	Congo (L.) Burundi
Shona	2 million	So. Rhodesia, Mozambique
Xhosa	2 million	South Africa
Kikuyu	1 million	Kenya
Kongo (*kiKongo*) . . .	1 million	Congo (L.), Congo (B.)
Ndongo (*kiNdongo*) . .	1 million	Angola
Nyamwesi-Sukuma . . .	1 million	Tanganyika
Nyanja	1 million	Nyasaland, No. Rhodesia
Thonga	1 million	Mozambique
Tswana	1 million	So. Africa, So. Rhodesia
Bemba	900,000	No. Rhodesia
Lingala	700,000	Congo (L.)

XVI. KHOIN (*5 languages*) 300,000

Hottentot (*nama*) . . .	200,000	South-West Africa
Bushman (*san*)	50,000	South-West Africa

OCEANIA

XVII. MALAYO-POLYNESIAN

(about 500 languages) . . . . 130 million

A. WESTERN . . . . 130 million

Javanese	45 million	Indonesia (Java)
Malay-Indonesian . . .	17 million	Indonesia, Malaya
Sundanese	14 million	Indonesia (Java)
Visayan	11 million	Philippines
Madurese	7 million	Indonesia (Madura)
Tagalog	6 million	Philippines
Malagasy	5 million	Malagasy
Ilocano (iloko)	3 million	Philippines
Balinese	2 million	Indonesia (Bali)
Batak	2 million	Indonesia (Sumatra)
Bikol	2 million	Philippines
Bugi	2 million	Indonesia (Celebes)
Dayak	1 million	Indonesia (Borneo), Sarawak

B. EASTERN . . . . 1 million

Fiji . . . . 100,000 Fiji

Samoan	100,000	Western Samoa, Amer. Samoa
Maori	75,000	New Zealand
Tongan	70,000	Tonga
Chamorro	30,000	Guam
Tahitian	30,000	Tahiti
Hawaiian	25,000	Hawaii
Ponapese	10,000	Ponape
Yapese	7,000	Yap

XVIII. PAPUAN (*about 150 languages*) . . . 2 million

Bentoeni	100,000	West New Guinea
Ono	4,000	North-East New Guinea

XIX. AUSTRALIAN (*about 100 languages*) . . . 200,000

Worora	1,000	Australia (NW)

AMERICA

XX. AMERINDIAN (*about 700 languages*) . . 12 million

A. NORTH AMERICAN (*about 200 languages*) . . 2 million

1. *ESKIMO-ALEUT* 60,000

Eskimo (*inuit*)	50,000	Greenland, Alaska

2. *ATHABASCAN* 100,000

    Navaho . . . .   80,000 USA (N. Mex., Ariz.)

    Apache . . . .   5,000 USA (N. Mex., Tex.)

3. *ALGONQUIAN* 80,000

    Ojibwa . . . .   40,000 USA (Minn.), Canada

4. *PENUTIAN* . . . . . .   20,000 USA (Calif.)

5. *HOKA-SIOUAN* 70,000

    Cherokee . . . . . .   40,000 USA (N.C.)

6. *UTO-AZTECAN* . . . . 1 million

    Nahuatl . . . .   800,000 Mexico

B. Latin American *(about 500 languages)* . . 10 million

    Quechua . . . .   6 million Peru, Bolivia

    Aymara . . . .   1 million Peru, Bolivia

    Guarani . . . .   1 million Paraguay, Brazil

    Maya . . . .   1 million Mexico, Guatemala

    Arawak . . . .   200,000 Venezuela, Brit. Guiana

    Carib . . . .   200,000 Brazil, West Indies

SYNOPSIS

		Languages		Native Speakers	
EUROPE					
I	Indo-European	140		1,580,000,000	
II	Caucasian	25		5,000,000	
III	Basque	1	166	800,000	1,585,800,000
ASIA					
IV	Sino-Tibetan	30		760,000,000	
V	Semito-Hamitic	20		125,000,000	
VI	Dravidian	10		120,000,000	
VII	Japanese	1		95,000,000	
VIII	Uralic-Altaic	40		90,000,000	
IX	Southeast Asian	20		45,000,000	
X	Korean	1		37,000,000	
XI	Burushaski	1		20,000	
XII	Paleo-Siberian	6		20,000	
XIII	Ainu	1		10,000	
XIV	Andamanese	1	131	400	1,272,050,400
AFRICA					
XV	African	700		160,000,000	
XVI	Khoin	5	705	300,000	160,300,000
OCEANIA					
XVII	Malayo-Polynesian	500		130,000,000	
XVIII	Papuan	150		2,000,000	
XIX	Australian	100	750	200,000	132,200,000
AMERICA					
XX	Amerindian		700		12,000,000
	TOTAL		2,452		3,162,350,400
	Unclassified (c. 2%)		48		62,649,600
	TOTAL		2,500		3,225,000,000

APPENDIX B

Numerical Listing of Living Languages

All languages mentioned in the text are included here. For every language, the country with the largest number of its speakers is given. A second country is listed if mention seems warranted by a relatively large concentration of that language's speakers. No implication should be drawn that there may not be additional countries with sizable numbers of speakers; for such information the reader is referred to the text.

Chinese-Mandarin	515 million	China (N)
English	265 million	USA, UK
Hindi-Urdu	185 million	India (N), Pakistan
Spanish	145 million	Mexico, Spain
Russian	135 million	USSR
German	100 million	Germany, Austria
Japanese	95 million	Japan
Arabic	90 million	Egypt, Morocco
Bengali	85 million	Pakistan, India (E)
Portuguese	85 million	Brazil, Portugal
French	65 million	France, Canada
Cantonese	55 million	China (Canton)
Italian	55 million	Italy

Wu	55 million	China (Shanghai)
Fukienese	50 million	China (Fukien), Taiwan
Javanese	45 million	Indonesia (Java)
Telugu	42 million	India (S)
Ukrainian	38 million	USSR (Ukrainian SSR)
Korean	37 million	Korea
Punjabi	37 million	Pakistan, India (NW)
Tamil	37 million	India (S), Ceylon
Marathi	35 million	India (W)
Polish	33 million	Poland, USA
Vietnamese	31 million	Viet Nam
Turkish	27 million	Turkey
Thai	24 million	Thailand, China (Yunnan)
Gujarati	22 million	India (W)
Hakka	20 million	China (Kwangtung)
Rumanian	20 million	Rumania, USSR (Mold. SSR)
Burmese	18 million	Burma
Dutch-Flemish	17 million	Netherlands, Belgium
Kanarese	17 million	India (S)
Malay-Indonesian	17 million	Indonesia, Malaya
Malayalam	15 million	India (S)
Oriya	15 million	India (E)
Persian	15 million	Iran, Afghanistan
Rajasthani	15 million	India (W)
Serbo-Croatian	15 million	Yugoslavia

Pashto	14 million	Afghanistan, Pakistan
Sundanese	14 million	Indonesia (Java)
Hungarian	12 million	Hungary, Rumania
Swahili	11 million	Tanganyika, Kenya
Visayan	11 million	Philippines
Czech	10 million	Czechoslovakia
Greek	10 million	Greece
Hausa	9 million	Nigeria, Niger
Swedish	9 million	Sweden, USA
Nepali	8 million	Nepal, India (N)
Sinhalese	8 million	Ceylon
Amharic	7 million	Ethiopia
Azerbaijani	7 million	Iran, USSR (Azerbaijan SSR)
Bulgarian	7 million	Bulgaria
Byelorussian	7 million	USSR (Byelorussian SSR)
Madurese	7 million	Indonesia (Madura)
Tibetan	7 million	China (Tibet)
Uzbek	7 million	USSR (Uzbek SSR)
Assamese	6 million	India (E)
Berber	6 million	Morocco, Algeria
Fula	6 million	Nigeria, Guinea
Galla	6 million	Ethiopia, Kenya
Quechua	6 million	Peru, Bolivia
Tagalog	6 million	Philippines
Cambodian	5 million	Cambodia
Catalan	5 million	Spain

Danish	5 million	Denmark
Finnish	5 million	Finland
French Creole	5 million	Haiti
Ibo	5 million	Nigeria
Kazakh	5 million	USSR (Kazakh SSR), China
Kurdish	5 million	Turkey, Iran
Malagasy	5 million	Malagasy
Ruanda	5 million	Rwanda, Congo (L.)
Tatar	5 million	USSR (Tatar ASSR)
Yoruba	5 million	Nigeria
Armenian	4 million	USSR (Armenian SSR)
Mandingo	4 million	Mali, Ivory Coast
Norwegian	4 million	Norway, USA
Sindhi	4 million	Pakistan
Slovak	4 million	Czechoslovakia
Sotho	4 million	South Africa
Twi-Fante	4 million	Ghana
Uighur	4 million	China (Sinkiang)
Yiddish	4 million	USA (N. Y.), Israel
Zulu	4 million	South Africa
Afrikaans	3 million	South Africa
Albanian	3 million	Albania, Yugoslavia
Georgian	3 million	USSR (Georgian SSR)
Ilocano	3 million	Philippines
Lithuanian	3 million	USSR (Lithuanian SSR)

Lolo	3 million	China (Czechwan, Yunnan)
Luba	3 million	Congo (L.)
Miao	3 million	China (Kweichow, Hunan)
Mossi	3 million	Upper Volta, Mali
Santali	3 million	India (E)
Somali	3 million	Somalia, Ethiopia
Balinese	2 million	Indonesia (Bali)
Batak	2 million	Indonesia (Sumatra)
Bikol	2 million	Philippines
Bugi	2 million	Indonesia (Celebes)
Fang-Bulu	2 million	Cameroun, Gabon
Ganda	2 million	Uganda
Kanuri	2 million	Nigeria, Chad
Kashmiri	2 million	India (W), Pakistan
Lao	2 million	Laos
Makua	2 million	Mozambique
Mbundu	2 million	Angola
Rundi	2 million	Congo (L.), Burundi
Shan	2 million	Burma, China (Yunnan)
Shona	2 million	So. Rhodesia, Mozambique
Slovenian	2 million	Yugoslavia
Xhosa	2 million	South Africa
Aymara	1 million	Peru, Bolivia
Baluchi	1 million	Pakistan

Bhili	1 million	India (W)
Breton	1 million	France
Chuvash	1 million	USSR (Chuvash ASSR)
Dayak	1 million	Indonesia (Borneo), Sarawak
Efik	1 million	Nigeria
Estonian	1 million	USSR (Estonian SSR)
Ewe	1 million	Togo, Dahomey
Gaelic	1 million	Ireland
Gondi	1 million	India (E)
Guarani	1 million	Paraguay, Brazil
Hebrew	1 million	Israel
Khalkha	1 million	Mongolia
Kikuyu	1 million	Kenya
Kirgiz	1 million	USSR (Kirgiz SSR)
Kongo	1 million	Congo (L.), Congo (B.)
Latvian	1 million	USSR (Latvian SSR)
Macedonian	1 million	Yugoslavia
Maya	1 million	Mexico, Guatemala
Mende	1 million	Sierra Leone
Mordvin	1 million	USSR (Mordovian ASSR)
Ndongo	1 million	Angola
Nubian	1 million	Sudan
Nyamwesi-Sukuma	1 million	Tanganyika
Nyanja	1 million	Nyasaland, No. Rhodesia
Romany	1 million	Hungary, Spain
Sardinian	1 million	Italy (Sardinia)

Tadzhik	1 million	USSR (Tadzhik SSR)
Thonga	1 million	Mozambique
Tswana	1 million	South Africa, So. Rhodesia
Turkoman	1 million	USSR (Turkmen SSR)
Welsh	1 million	UK (Wales), USA
Bemba	900,000	No. Rhodesia
Basque	800,000	Spain, France
Fon	800,000	Dahomey
Nahuatl	800,000	Mexico
Kpelle	700,000	Liberia, Guinea
Lingala	700,000	Congo (L.)
Rhaeto-Romanic	600,000	Italy, Switzerland
Bini	500,000	Nigeria
Tigrinya	500,000	Ethiopia
Chechen	400,000	USSR (Checheno-Ingush SSR)
Frisian	300,000	Netherlands
Luxemburgian	300,000	Luxemburg
Mon	300,000	Burma
Aramaic-Syriac	200,000	Turkey, Iraq
Arawak	200,000	Venezuela, Brit. Guiana
Brahui	200,000	Pakistan
Carib	200,000	Brazil, West Indies
Hottentot	200,000	South-West Africa
Kabardin	200,000	USSR (Kabardinian ASSR)
Manchu	200,000	China (Manchuria)

Papiamento	200,000	Netherlands Antilles
Portuguese Creole	200,000	Cape Verde Islands
Icelandic	160,000	Iceland, Faroe Islands
Ladino	140,000	Turkey, Greece
Bentoeni	100,000	West New Guinea
Circassian	100,000	USSR (Cherkess ASSR)
Fiji	100,000	Fiji
Lusatian	100,000	Germany
Samoan	100,000	Western Samoa, Amer. Samoa
Scottish Gaelic	100,000	UK (Scotland)
Tigre	100,000	Ethiopia
Navaho	80,000	USA (N.Mex., Ariz.)
Maori	75,000	New Zealand
Abkhaz	70,000	USSR (Abkhazian SSR)
Tongan	70,000	Tonga
Bushman	50,000	South-West Africa
Eskimo	50,000	Greenland, Alaska
South Arabic	50,000	Muscat and Oman
Cherokee	40,000	USA (N.C.)
Lapp	40,000	Norway, Sweden
Ojibwa	40,000	USA (Minn.), Canada
Chamorro	30,000	Guam
Tahitian	30,000	Tahiti
Hawaiian	25,000	Hawaii
Samoyed	22,000	USSR (W Siberia)
Burushaski	20,000	Pakistan

Penutian	20,000	USA (Cal.)
Tungus	15,000	USSR (E Siberia)
Chukchee	11,000	USSR (NE Siberia)
Ainu	10,000	Japan
Ponapese	10,000	Ponape
Yapese	7,000	Yap
Apache	5,000	USA (N.Mex., Tex.)
Ono	4,000	North-East New Guinea
Worora	1,000	Australia (NW)
Andamanese	400	India (Andaman Islands)

APPENDIX C

Geographical Distribution of Native Speakers

Only languages mentioned in the text are listed here. Sequence is alphabetical by countries and numerical under each country. The numbers in parentheses are estimated population figures as of January 1, 1964. They are expressed in millions, rounded off to the nearest million for populations over three million, and to the nearest ten or hundred thousand for smaller populations. Languages in capital letters have official status. Where a language is spoken in only one country, the number of speakers is rounded off as described in the Preface.

Aden (1.3)	Arabic	1,300,000
	ENGLISH	10,000
Afghanistan (16)	PASHTO	8,000,000
	PERSIAN	3,000,000
	Uzbek	800,000
	Turkoman	200,000
Albania (1.9)	ALBANIAN	1,900,000
	Greek	10,000
Algeria (12)	ARABIC	9,000,000
	Berber	2,000,000
	FRENCH	1,000,000

American Samoa (0.02)	ENGLISH	10,000
	Samoan	10,000
Andorra (0.01)	CATALAN	10,000
Angola (5)	Mbundu	2,000,000
	Ndongo	1,000,000
	PORTUGUESE	1,000,000
Argentina (22)	SPANISH	16,000,000
	Italian	1,200,000
	German	600,000
	Quechua	200,000
	Yiddish	200,000
Australia (11)	ENGLISH	11,000,000
	German	150,000
	Worora	1,000
Australia: Trust Territory of New Guinea (1.6)	ENGLISH	300,000
	Ono	4,000
Austria (7)	GERMAN	7,000,000
	Slovenian	20,000
Bahrein (0.2)	ARABIC	200,000
Basutoland (0.7)	ENGLISH	500,000
	Sotho	100,000
	Afrikaans	60,000
Bechuanaland (0.4)	ENGLISH	200,000
	Afrikaans	140,000
	Tswana	40,000
Belgium (9)	FLEMISH	5,000,000
	FRENCH	4,000,000
	German	180,000

Bhutan (0.7)	TIBETAN	650,000
	Nepali	15,000
Bolivia (4)	SPANISH	1,600,000
	Quechua	1,600,000
	Aymara	400,000
Brazil (79)	PORTUGUESE	72,000,000
	German	700,000
	Italian	500,000
	Guarani	300,000
	Quechua	300,000
	Japanese	200,000
	Carib	100,000
British African isles (0.7)	French Creole	300,000
	ENGLISH	100,000
	Hindustani	100,000
	Swahili	50,000
British Guiana (0.6)	Arawak	50,000
	ENGLISH	20,000
British Honduras (0.1)	ENGLISH	40,000
	Maya	10,000
British Pacific isles (0.7)	ENGLISH	200,000
	Fiji	100,000
	Hindustani	100,000
	Tongan	70,000
British West Indies isles (0.9)	ENGLISH	700,000
	Carib	100,000
	Arawak	30,000
Brunei (0.1)	Malay	50,000
	ENGLISH	2,000

Bulgaria (8)	BULGARIAN	7,000,000
	Macedonian	200,000
	Turkish	200,000
	Romany	150,000
	Rumanian	100,000
	Armenian	50,000
	Greek	50,000
	Ladino	10,000
Burma (24)	BURMESE	18,000,000
	Shan	1,500,000
	Cantonese	400,000
	Mon	300,000
Burundi (2.9)	Rundi	800,000
	Swahili	500,000
	FRENCH	200,000
Cambodia (6)	CAMBODIAN	5,000,000
	Vietnamese	280,000
	Cantonese	250,000
	FRENCH	50,000
Cameroun (5)	Fang-Bulu	1,500,000
	Fula	600,000
	Hausa	300,000
	FRENCH	200,000
	ENGLISH	5,000
Canada (19)	ENGLISH	13,000,000
	FRENCH	5,000,000
	German	500,000
	Ukrainian	400,000
	Polish	130,000
	Italian	100,000
	Swedish	100,000
	Yiddish	100,000

	Ojibwa	20,000
	Scottish Gaelic	10,000
	Eskimo	9,000
Canal Zone (0.05)	ENGLISH	20,000
	Spanish	20,000
Cape Verde Islands (0.2)	Portuguese Creole	150,000
	PORTUGUESE	10,000
Central African Republic (1.3)	FRENCH	150,000
Ceylon (11)	SINHALESE	8,000,000
	Tamil	3,000,000
Chad (2.8)	Arabic	1,500,000
	Kanuri	350,000
	Berber	200,000
	FRENCH	100,000
Chile (8)	SPANISH	7,500,000
	German	100,000
	Quechua	100,000
China, Nationalist (12)	Fukienese	9,000,000
	CHINESE-MANDARIN	1,500,000
	Japanese	500,000
	Malay	100,000
China, People's Republic (730)	CHINESE-MANDARIN	515,000,000
	Wu	56,000,000
	Cantonese	46,000,000
	Fukienese	36,000,000
	Hakka	20,000,000
	Tibetan	6,000,000
	Uighur*	4,000,000
	Lolo	3,000,000

* Official in Turkistan.

	Miao	3,000,000
	Thai	2,000,000
	Kazakh	600,000
	Shan	500,000
	Manchu	200,000
Colombia (15)	SPANISH	13,000,000
	German	200,000
Comoro Islands (0.2)	Swahili	150,000
	FRENCH	30,000
Congo (Brazzaville) (0.9)	Kongo	300,000
	FRENCH	200,000
Congo (Leopoldville)	Luba	3,000,000
(15)	Ruanda	2,500,000
	Swahili	2,000,000
	Rundi	1,200,000
	FRENCH	1,000,000
	Kongo	1,000,000
	Lingala	700,000
Costa Rica (1.4)	SPANISH	1,200,000
	English	20,000
Cuba (7)	SPANISH	7,000,000
Cyprus (0.6)	GREEK	450,000
	TURKISH	110,000
	Armenian	5,000
Czechoslovakia (14)	CZECH	9,000,000
	SLOVAK	4,000,000
	Hungarian	400,000
	Romany	150,000
	German	100,000

Dahomey (2.4)	Fon	800,000
	Ewe	400,000
	FRENCH	250,000
	Yoruba	150,000
	Hausa	100,000
	Fula	70,000
Denmark (5)	DANISH	4,700,000
	German	10,000
Dominican Republic (3)	SPANISH	3,000,000
	French Creole	10,000
Ecuador (5)	SPANISH	4,000,000
	Quechua	350,000
El Salvador (2.8)	SPANISH	2,700,000
	Nahuatl	20,000
Ethiopia (22)	AMHARIC	7,000,000
	Galla	5,000,000
	Somali	1,000,000
	Tigrinya	500,000
	Arabic	200,000
	Tigre	100,000
	ENGLISH	10,000
Faroe Islands (0.04)	ICELANDIC (FAROESE)	30,000
Finland (5)	FINNISH	4,000,000
	SWEDISH	400,000
	Lapp	5,000
	Romany	2,000
France (48)	FRENCH	44,000,000
	German	1,800,000
	Breton	1,000,000
	Italian	1,000,000

	Arabic	200,000
	Catalan	200,000
	Basque	100,000
	Yiddish	100,000
	Armenian	30,000
	Flemish	20,000
French Guiana (0.04)	French Creole	30,000
	FRENCH	5,000
French Polynesia (0.08)	Tahitian	30,000
	FRENCH	10,000
French Somaliland (0.06)	Somali	50,000
	FRENCH	10,000
Gabon (0.5)	Fang-Bulu	250,000
	FRENCH	100,000
Gambia (0.3)	Fula	100,000
	Mandingo	80,000
	ENGLISH	50,000
Germany (75)	GERMAN	75,000,000
	Lusatian	100,000
	Frisian	17,000
	Danish	10,000
Ghana (8)	Twi-Fante	4,000,000
	ENGLISH	1,000,000
Gibraltar (0.03)	Spanish	20,000
	ENGLISH	10,000
Greece (9)	GREEK	8,000,000
	Turkish	200,000
	Albanian	100,000
	Macedonian	100,000
	Ladino	30,000

Greenland (0.04)	Eskimo	28,000
	DANISH	10,000
Guadeloupe (0.3)	French Creole	200,000
	FRENCH	50,000
Guam (0.07)	ENGLISH	40,000
	Chamorro	30,000
Guatemala (4)	SPANISH	1,600,000
	Maya	500,000
	Carib	3,000
Guinea (3)	Fula	1,000,000
	Mandingo	600,000
	FRENCH	100,000
	Kpelle	100,000
Haiti (5)	French Creole	4,000,000
	FRENCH	400,000
Honduras (2)	SPANISH	2,000,000
	Maya	100,000
Hong Kong (4)	Cantonese	3,500,000
	ENGLISH	20,000
Hungary (10)	HUNGARIAN	9,000,000
	German	300,000
	Romany	200,000
	Serbo-Croatian	50,000
	Slovak	50,000
Iceland (0.2)	ICELANDIC	130,000
	Danish	20,000
India (472)	HINDI-Urdu	165,000,000
	Telugu	42,000,000
	Bengali	37,000,000

	Marathi	35,000,000
	Tamil	33,000,000
	Gujarati	22,000,000
	Kanarese	17,000,000
	Punjabi	17,000,000
	Malayalam	15,000,000
	Oriya	15,000,000
	Rajasthani	15,000,000
	Assamese	6,000,000
	Santali	3,000,000
	ENGLISH	2,000,000
	Kashmiri	1,200,000
	Bhili	1,000,000
	Gondi	1,000,000
	Nepali	1,000,000
	Aramaic-Syriac	30,000
	Andamanese	400
Indonesia (103)	Javanese	45,000,000
	Sundanese	14,000,000
	MALAY-INDONESIAN	12,000,000
	Madurese	7,000,000
	Fukienese	2,800,000
	Balinese	2,000,000
	Batak	2,000,000
	Bugi	2,000,000
	Dayak	800,000
	Bentoeni	100,000
Iran (22)	PERSIAN	12,000,000
	Azerbaijani	4,000,000
	Kurdish	1,500,000
	Armenian	300,000
	Baluchi	100,000
	Aramaic-Syriac	40,000
	Brahui	30,000

Iraq (8)	ARABIC	6,500,000
	Kurdish	1,000,000
	Turkoman	70,000
	Aramaic-Syriac	50,000
	Armenian	50,000
	Persian	50,000
Ireland (2.8)	ENGLISH	1,900,000
	GAELIC	900,000
Israel (2.4)	HEBREW	1,100,000
	Yiddish	800,000
	ARABIC	220,000
	German	100,000
	Ladino	20,000
Italy (51)	ITALIAN	49,000,000
	Sardinian	1,000,000
	Rhaeto-Romanic	520,000
	German*	450,000
	French	300,000
	Albanian	100,000
	Slovenian	20,000
Ivory Coast (3)	Mandingo	1,000,000
	FRENCH	200,000
Jamaica (1.7)	ENGLISH	1,700,000
Japan (96)	JAPANESE	95,000,000
	Korean	600,000
	Ainu	10,000
Jordan (1.8)	ARABIC	1,700,000
	Armenian	50,000

* Co-official in Alto Adige.

Kenya (9)	Swahili	2,500,000
	ENGLISH	1,500,000
	Kikuyu	1,200,000
	Galla	500,000
Korea (36)	KOREAN	36,000,000
Kuwait (0.3)	ARABIC	300,000
Laos (2)	LAO	1,500,000
	FRENCH	100,000
	Vietnamese	50,000
	Cantonese	30,000
Lebanon (2)	ARABIC	1,800,000
	Armenian	100,000
	French	100,000
Liberia (1.3)	Kpelle	600,000
	ENGLISH	300,000
	Mandingo	300,000
Libya (1.3)	ARABIC	1,000,000
	Berber	300,000
Liechtenstein (0.02)	GERMAN	17,000
Luxemburg (0.3)	LUXEMBURGIAN	300,000
	FRENCH	20,000
Macao (0.2)	Cantonese	170,000
	PORTUGUESE	10,000
Malagasy (6)	MALAGASY	5,000,000
	FRENCH	700,000
Malaya (8)	MALAY	4,200,000
	Fukienese	2,500,000
	Tamil	800,000
	Arabic	50,000
	English	50,000

Maldive Islands (0.1)	SINHALESE	90,000
Mali (4)	Mandingo	1,400,000
	FRENCH	500,000
	Fula	400,000
	Mossi	400,000
Malta (0.3)	ARABIC (MALTESE)	200,000
	ENGLISH	30,000
Martinique (0.3)	French Creole	200,000
	FRENCH	50,000
Mauritania (0.8)	Arabic	600,000
	Berber	100,000
	FRENCH	100,000
Mexico (39)	SPANISH	35,000,000
	Nahuatl	800,000
	Maya	600,000
	German	200,000
	Yiddish	200,000
Monaco (0.02)	FRENCH	20,000
Mongolia (1)	KHALKHA	900,000
	Kazakh	50,000
Morocco (13)	ARABIC	10,000,000
	Berber	2,000,000
	French	100,000
	Spanish	100,000
Mount Athos (0.006)	GREEK	5,000
Mozambique (7)	PORTUGUESE	2,000,000
	Makua	1,500,000
	Thonga	1,300,000
	Shona	300,000

Muscat and Oman (0.6)	ARABIC	500,000
	South Arabic	50,000
	Hindi	20,000
Nauru (0.005)	ENGLISH	5,000
Nepal (10)	NEPALI	7,000,000
	Hindi	1,500,000
	Tibetan	200,000
Netherlands (12)	DUTCH	12,000,000
	Frisian	250,000
Netherlands Antilles (0.2)	Papiamento	200,000
	DUTCH	5,000
New Caledonia (0.08)	FRENCH	25,000
New Hebrides (0.07)	ENGLISH	20,000
	FRENCH	20,000
New Zealand (2.6)	ENGLISH	2,500,000
	Maori	75,000
Nicaragua (1.7)	SPANISH	1,600,000
Niger (3)	Berber	1,000,000
	Hausa	1,000,000
	FRENCH	500,000
	Fula	200,000
	Arabic	100,000
	Kanuri	100,000
Nigeria (37)	Hausa*	7,000,000
	Ibo	5,000,000
	Yoruba	5,000,000
	Fula	3,000,000
	Kanuri	1,500,000

* Official in North Region.

	Efik	1,000,000
	ENGLISH	1,000,000
	Bini	500,000
North Borneo (0.5)	Malay	200,000
	Fukienese	100,000
	ENGLISH	10,000
Northern Rhodesia (2.7)	Bemba	900,000
	ENGLISH	300,000
	Nyanja	300,000
Norway (4)	NORWEGIAN	3,600,000
	Lapp	25,000
Nyasaland (3)	Nyanja	1,000,000
	ENGLISH	300,000
Pakistan (100)	BENGALI	47,000,000
	Punjabi	20,000,000
	URDU	20,000,000
	Pashto	6,000,000
	Sindhi	4,000,000
	Kashmiri	1,000,000
	Baluchi	800,000
	ENGLISH	500,000
	Gujarati	250,000
	Brahui	200,000
	Burushaski	20,000
Panama (1.2)	SPANISH	1,100,000
	English	60,000
Papua (0.6)	ENGLISH	50,000
Paraguay (1.8)	SPANISH	1,000,000
	Guarani	800,000

Peru (12)	SPANISH	6,000,000
	Quechua	3,500,000
	Aymara	800,000
Philippines (31)	Visayan	11,000,000
	TAGALOG	6,000,000
	Ilocano	3,000,000
	Bikol	2,000,000
	Spanish	500,000
	Fukienese	300,000
	English	50,000
Poland (31)	POLISH	29,000,000
	German	1,000,000
	Yiddish	50,000
Portugal (9)	PORTUGUESE	9,000,000
Portuguese Guinea (0.6)	Fula	300,000
	Portuguese Creole	50,000
	PORTUGUESE	10,000
Portuguese Timor (0.5)	PORTUGUESE	5,000
Puerto Rico (2.5)	SPANISH	2,300,000
	ENGLISH	200,000
Qatar (0.06)	ARABIC	60,000
Réunion (0.4)	FRENCH	100,000
	French Creole	100,000
Rumania (19)	RUMANIAN	17,000,000
	Hungarian*	600,000
	German	400,000
	Bulgarian	200,000
	Yiddish	150,000
	Romany	70,000
	Armenian	50,000

* Co-official in Transylvania.

Rwanda (2.9)	Ruanda	2,600,000
	FRENCH	200,000
Ryukyu Islands (0.9)	Japanese	800,000
	ENGLISH	20,000
San Marino (0.02)	ITALIAN	20,000
San Tome and Principe (0.07)	PORTUGUESE	10,000
Sarawak (0.8)	Dayak	300,000
	Fukienese	200,000
	Malay	200,000
	ENGLISH	50,000
Saudi Arabia (7)	ARABIC	7,000,000
Senegal (3)	Fula	600,000
	Mandingo	400,000
	FRENCH	150,000
Sierra Leone (2.6)	Mende	1,100,000
	ENGLISH	600,000
Sikkim (0.2)	Nepali	150,000
	ENGLISH	20,000
Singapore (1.9)	Fukienese	1,100,000
	Malay	400,000
	ENGLISH	300,000
	Tamil	100,000
Somalia (2.1)	SOMALI	1,800,000
	Arabic	200,000
	Italian	5,000
South Africa (17)	Sotho	3,500,000
	Zulu	3,500,000
	AFRIKAANS	2,250,000

	Xhosa	2,000,000
	ENGLISH	1,000,000
	Tswana	1,000,000
	Tamil	100,000
Southern Rhodesia (4)	Shona	2,000,000
	ENGLISH	500,000
	Zulu	400,000
	Tswana	300,000
South-West Africa (0.6)	ENGLISH	200,000
	Hottentot	200,000
	Bushman	50,000
Spain (31)	SPANISH	23,000,000
	Catalan	5,000,000
	Portuguese	2,000,000
	Basque	700,000
	Romany	200,000
Spain: Equatorial African territories (0.3)	Fang-Bulu	200,000
	SPANISH	20,000
Spain: North African territories (0.2)	SPANISH	100,000
	Arabic	100,000
Sudan (13)	ARABIC	8,000,000
	Nubian	1,000,000
Surinam (0.4)	English	80,000
	Arawak	40,000
	DUTCH	20,000
Swaziland (0.3)	ENGLISH	100,000
	Afrikaans	50,000
Sweden (8)	SWEDISH	7,500,000
	Finnish	30,000
	Lapp	10,000

Switzerland (6)	GERMAN	4,000,000
	FRENCH	1,300,000
	ITALIAN	400,000
	RHAETO-ROMANIC	40,000
Syria (5)	ARABIC	4,200,000
	Armenian	300,000
	Kurdish	300,000
	Circassian	5,000
	Aramaic-Syriac	4,000
Tanganyika (10)	Swahili	5,500,000
	ENGLISH	1,500,000
	Nyamwesi-Sukuma	1,000,000
Thailand (29)	THAI	21,000,000
	Cantonese	3,000,000
	Malay	200,000
	Vietnamese	80,000
Togo (1.6)	Ewe	600,000
	Hausa	200,000
	Twi-Fante	200,000
	FRENCH	100,000
Trinidad and Tobago (0.9)	ENGLISH	700,000
	Arawak	20,000
Trucial Oman (0.1)	ARABIC	100,000
Tunisia (4)	ARABIC	3,500,000
	Berber	500,000
Turkey (30)	TURKISH	26,000,000
	Kurdish	2,000,000
	Greek	500,000
	Arabic	300,000
	Armenian	300,000
	Ladino	80,000

	Aramaic-Syriac	60,000
	Georgian	50,000
	Circassian	10,000
Uganda (7)	GANDA	1,500,000
	ENGLISH	1,000,000
	Swahili	200,000
Union of Soviet Socialist Republics (227)	RUSSIAN	133,000,000
	UKRAINIAN	37,000,000
	BYELORUSSIAN	7,400,000
	Uzbek	6,600,000
	Tatar	5,200,000
	Kazakh	3,900,000
	Azerbaijani	3,200,000
	Armenian	2,800,000
	Georgian	2,700,000
	Lithuanian	2,600,000
	Rumanian	2,400,000
	Latvian	1,300,000
	German	1,200,000
	Chuvash	1,000,000
	Estonian	1,000,000
	Kirgiz	1,000,000
	Mordvin	1,000,000
	Tadzhik	1,000,000
	Turkoman	1,000,000
	Polish	650,000
	Yiddish	500,000
	Chechen	400,000
	Bulgarian	250,000
	Kabardin	200,000
	Circassian	100,000
	Greek	100,000
	Swedish	100,000
	Romany	80,000
	Uighur	80,000

	Abkhaz	70,000
	Kurdish	70,000
	Samoyed	22,000
	Aramaic-Syriac	20,000
	Tungus	15,000
	Chukchee	11,000
	Eskimo	1,000
United Arab Republic (29)	ARABIC	28,000,000
	Armenian	100,000
United Kingdom (55)	ENGLISH	54,000,000
	Welsh	700,000
	Scottish Gaelic	100,000
	French*	100,000
	Gaelic	50,000
United States (191)	ENGLISH	165,000,000
	German	4,500,000
	Italian	3,500,000
	Polish	3,000,000
	Spanish†	3,000,000
	Yiddish	2,000,000
	Russian	1,500,000
	French	1,300,000
	Czech	900,000
	Swedish	900,000
	Ukrainian	800,000
	Norwegian	700,000
	Hungarian	500,000
	Danish	400,000
	Greek	400,000
	Finnish	300,000
	Lithuanian	300,000
	Serbo-Croatian	300,000

* Co-official on Jersey.
† Co-official in New Mexico.

	Welsh	300,000
	Dutch	240,000
	Portuguese	200,000
	Albanian	100,000
	Armenian	100,000
	Cantonese	100,000
	Rumanian	100,000
	Slovenian	100,000
	Navaho	80,000
	Cherokee	40,000
	Frisian	30,000
	Hawaiian	25,000
	Ojibwa	20,000
	Penutian	20,000
	Eskimo	10,000
	Apache	5,000
United States: Trust Territory of the Pacific Islands (0.09)	ENGLISH	10,000
	Ponapese	10,000
	Yapese	7,000
Upper Volta (5)	Mossi	3,000,000
	FRENCH	200,000
	Fula	200,000
Uruguay (3)	SPANISH	2,500,000
Vatican City (0.001)	ITALIAN	1,000
Venezuela (8)	SPANISH	7,200,000
	Arawak	80,000
Viet Nam (33)	VIETNAMESE	30,500,000
	Cantonese	900,000
	Thai	500,000
	Cambodian	300,000
	French	100,000

Virgin Islands (US) (0.04)	ENGLISH	30,000
Western Samoa (0.1)	Samoan	100,000
	ENGLISH	1,000
Yemen (5)	ARABIC	5,000,000
Yugoslavia (20)	SERBO-CROATIAN	15,000,000
	Slovenian	1,600,000
	Macedonian	1,000,000
	Albanian	600,000
	Hungarian	500,000
	German	300,000
	Italian	300,000
	Turkish	250,000
	Romany	140,000
Zanzibar (0.3)	Swahili	300,000
	ENGLISH	5,000

GLOSSARY

Only linguistic terms occurring in the text and not explained there are listed. Definitions are limited to the sense in which the terms are used in the text. The derivation is given in parentheses. Abbreviations: *a*—adjective, F—French, G—German, Gr—Greek, H—Hebrew, L—Latin, *n*—noun, *v*—verb.

accent (L *ad,* "to" + *cantus,* "song") *n:* a mark placed above or next to a letter to indicate a change in sound or meaning.

acute (L *acutus,* "sharp") *n:* an accent having the form ′.

adscript (L *ad,* "to" + *scriptus,* "written") *a:* added to a letter in writing.

affix (L *ad,* "to" + *fixus,* "attached") *n:* a letter or group of letters attached to or inserted within a word stem to produce a derivative.

affricate (L *ad,* "to" + *fricatus,* "rubbed") *n:* a stop sound followed immediately by a continuant; affrication *n:* conversion into an affricate.

agglutinative (L *ad,* "to" + *glutinare,* "glue") *a:* combining into a single word several elements, each of which is a separate entity, usually an affix.

alveolar (L *alveus,* "cavity") *a:* articulated with the tip of the tongue approaching the upper toothridge.

analytic (Gr *ana,* "back" + *lyo,* "loose") *a:* dissolving into component elements and thus eliminating the need for inflections. Antonym: synthetic.

aspirate (L *ad,* "upon" + *spirare,* "breathe") *v:* to pronounce with an *h* sound; *n:* 1) a combination of letters or sounds of which the last is an *h;* 2) an intensive expulsion of breath after a stop sound; aspiration *n:* such pronunciation.

back vowel: a vowel produced by the tongue's being arched toward the rear part of the mouth's roof, notably *o* and *u.* Synonym: velar vowel. Antonyms: front vowel, palatal vowel.

bilabial (L *bi,* "two" + *labium,* "lip") *a:* articulated with both lips.

cacuminal (L *cacumen,* "point") *a:* produced with the tongue tip turned toward the hard palate. Synonym: retroflex.

cardinal vowel: a vowel sound produced with well-defined position of the speech organs to serve as a standard with which to compare vowels in different languages.

cedilla (diminutive of Gr *zeta,* "zee") *n:* a mark attached to the bottom of some letters, notably *c,* to indicate a change in pronunciation.

circumflex (L *circum,* "around" + *flexus,* "bent") *n:* an accent having the form ^ , ^ , or ~ .

cognate (L *con,* "together" + *natus,* "born") *n:* a word related to one in another language by descent from a common ancestral language.

continuant (L *continuare,* "continue") *n:* a consonant whose duration may be prolonged during one emission of breath. Antonym: stop.

cuneiform (L *cuneus,* "wedge" + F *forme,* "form") *a:* written in wedge-shaped characters.

dental (L *dens,* "tooth") *a*: articulated by the tip of the tongue touching the upper teeth or approaching the space between both rows of teeth.

diachronic (Gr *dia,* "through" + *chronos,* "time") *a*: historical, describing the changes which evolved in the course of time.

diacritic (Gr *dia,* "apart" + *krinein,* "distinguish") *n*: a mark indicating a modification in pronunciation or meaning as compared to an unmarked character.

diaeresis (Gr *dia,* "apart" + *hairein,* "take") *n*: a mark (") placed over a second vowel to indicate pronunciation in separate syllables.

digraph (Gr *di,* "twofold" + *grapho,* "write") *n*: a union of two characters representing one single sound.

diphthong (Gr *di,* "twofold" + *phthongos,* "voice") *n*: the combination of two vowels into a single syllable; diphthongization *n*: the change of a vowel into a diphthong.

enclitic (Gr *en,* "on" + *klitikos,* "leaning") *n*: a word or particle without independent accent, and attached to a preceding word.

etymological (Gr *etymon,* "true sense" + *logia,* "science") *a*: in accord with the history of the linguistic form of a word.

fricative (L *fricatus,* "rubbed") *n*: a consonant produced by passage of breath through a narrowed opening in the mouth. Synonym: spirant.

front vowel: a vowel produced by the tongue's being arched toward the front part of the mouth's roof, notably *e* and *i*. Synonym: palatal vowel. Antonyms: back vowel, velar vowel.

glottal (Gr *glotta,* "language") *a*: produced at the glottis, the space between the vocal folds. Synonym: laryngeal.

grammar (Gr *grammatike,* "letters") *n:* the study or description of the form and position of words in a language; grammatical *a.*

grave (L *gravis,* "heavy") *n:* an accent having the form

guttural (L *guttur,* "throat") *a:* formed with the back of the tongue approaching the velum, the soft palate. Synonym: velar.

hieroglyphics (Gr *hieros,* "sacred" + *glyphein,* "carve") *n:* the picture script of the ancient Egyptian priesthood.

homonym (Gr *homo,* "alike" + *onyma,* "name") *n:* a word written like another but differing in meaning.

homophone (Gr *homo,* "alike" + *phone,* "sound") *n:* a word pronounced like another but differing in meaning.

ideographic (Gr *idea,* "idea" + *graphos,* "written") *a:* representing an idea suggested by a written symbol.

infix (L *in,* "in" + *fixus,* "attached") *n:* a letter or group of letters inserted within a word stem; infixion *n:* word formation by means of an infix.

inflection (L *in,* "in" + *flectere,* "bend") *n:* 1) change in voice; 2) change of words to make grammatical distinctions; inflect *v;* inflectional *a.*

isolating (L *insula,* "island") *a:* having all words unchangeable and therefore requiring rigid syntax. Antonym: inflecting.

laryngeal (Gr *larynx,* "larynx") *a:* produced at the larynx. Synonym: glottal.

lexical (Gr *lexis,* "word") *a:* pertaining to the vocabulary.

ligature (L *ligare,* "bind") *n:* several characters united in one form.

liquid (L *liquidus,* "liquid") *n:* the consonants *l* and *r.*

macron (Gr *makros,* "long") *n:* a mark (¯) placed over a long vowel.

media (L *medius,* "middle") *n:* a voiced stop.

minuscule (diminutive of L *minor,* "smaller") *n:* lowercase. Antonym: majuscule.

monophthong (Gr *monos,* "alone" + *phthongos,* "sound") *n:* one single vowel.

morpheme (Gr *morphe,* "form") *n:* a smallest meaningful part of a word; morphemic *a.*

morphology (Gr *morphe,* "form" + *logia,* "science") *n:* the method or description of word formation; morphological *a.*

nasal (L *nasus,* "nose") *n:* a sound characterized by resonance produced through the nose; nasalize *v;* nasalization *n.*

palatal (L *palatum,* "palate") *a:* formed with the front or blade of the tongue approaching the hard palate, the roof of the mouth; palatalize *v:* to modify a nonpalatal sound by bringing the front of the tongue near the hard palate; palatalization *n:* such modification. Synonym: fronting.

phoneme (Gr *phone,* "sound") *n:* a smallest distinctive unit of speech; phonemic *a.*

phonetic (Gr *phone,* "sound") *a:* representing the sound by symbols of fixed value.

phonographic (Gr *phone,* "sound" + *graphos,* "written") *a:* reproducing the sound.

pictographic (L *pictor,* "painter" + Gr *graphos,* "written") *a:* representing a definite object or idea by a picture.

polysyllabic (Gr *poly,* "many" + *syllabe,* "syllable") *a:* having several syllables, usually more than three.

polysynthetic (Gr *poly,* "many" + *syn,* "together" + *tithenai,* "put") *a:* combining into a composite form, with resulting extended thought concept, various elements that do not have individual existence.

postpositive (L *post,* "after" + *ponere,* "put") *a:* placed after a word.

prefix (L *pre,* "in front of" + *fixus,* "attached") *n:* a letter or group of letters attached at the beginning of a word; prefixion *n:* word formation by means of a prefix.

retroflex (L *retro,* "back" + *flexus,* "bent") *a:* produced with the tongue tip turned up toward the hard palate. Synonym: cacuminal.

semantic (Gr *sema,* "sign") *a:* relating to meaning.

semiuncial (L *semi,* "half" + *uncia,* "inch") *n:* style of writing which developed in the eighth century.

shibboleth (H *shibboleth,* "ear of grain") *n:* a word serving as a test to detect a speaker's native tongue by his inability to pronounce a particular phoneme.

sibilant (L *sibilans,* "hissing") *n:* a fricative with a sound resembling that of *s.*

spirant (L *spirans,* "breathing") *n:* a consonant produced by passage of breath through a narrowed opening. Synonym: fricative.

stop *n:* a consonant articulated by a closure of the breath passage. Synonyms: occlusive, plosive, explosive. Antonym: continuant.

subscript (L *sub,* "under" + *scriptus,* "written") *a:* written under a letter.

substratal (L *sub,* "under" + *stratus,* "spread") *a:* underlying.

suffix (L *sub,* "close to" + *fixus,* "attached") *n:* a letter or group of letters attached to the end of a word; suffixion *n:* word formation by means of a suffix.

superscript (L *super,* "above" + *scriptus,* "written") *a:* written over a letter.

syllabary (Gr *syllabe,* "syllable") *n*: a listing of characters used to represent syllables.

synchronic (Gr *syn,* "together" + *chronos,* "time") *a*: contemporary, limited to the stage of development at the same given period of time. Antonym: diachronic.

syncopation (Gr *syn,* "together" + *koptein,* "cut") *n*: elimination of a sound or letter in the interior of a word.

synonym (Gr *syn,* "together" + *onyma,* "name") *n*: a word of like meaning.

syntax (Gr *syn,* "together" + *taxis,* "arrangement") *n*: the part of grammar dealing with the order of elements in phrases and sentences.

synthetic (Gr *syn,* "together" + *tithenai,* "put") *a*: using inflections to indicate grammatical relationships. Antonym: analytic.

tenuis (L *tenuis,* "slight") *n*: the voiceless consonants *p, t, k*.

triphthong (Gr *tri,* "three" + *phthongos,* "sound") *n*: a combination of three successive vowels.

umlaut (G *um,* "around" + *Laut,* "sound") *n*: a vowel resulting from the fronting or raising of a back or low vowel, indicated sometimes by the superscript mark ¨.

uvular (diminutive of L *uva,* "grape") *a*: produced with the aid of the uvula, the pendant portion of the soft palate.

velar (L *velum* "curtain") *a*: formed with the back of the tongue approaching the velum, the soft palate. Synonym: guttural.

voiced *a*: with the vibration of the vocal folds. Antonyms: voiceless, unvoiced, devoiced, breath(ed).

voiceless *a*: without vibration of the vocal folds. Synonyms: unvoiced, devoiced, breath(ed). Antonym: voiced.

world language: a language that at a given time is a means of communication between different speech communities to a larger extent than any other tongue.

BIBLIOGRAPHY

This list is highly selective and does not aim to be complete. Only those items that have a direct bearing on significant general aspects in the text are included.

Bloomfield, Leonard. *Language.* New York: Henry Holt and Co., 1933.

Bodmer, Frederick. *The Loom of Language.* New York: W. W. Norton & Co., 1944.

Brosnahan, L. F. *The Sounds of Language.* Cambridge, England: W. Heffer & Sons, 1961.

Bryan, M. A. *The Bantu Languages of Africa.* London: Oxford University Press, 1959.

Carroll, John B. *The Study of Language.* Cambridge: Harvard University Press, 1961.

De Bray, R. G. A. *Guide to the Slavonic Languages.* New York: E. P. Dutton & Co., 1951.

Diringer, David. *The Alphabet.* New York: Philosophical Library, 1948.
————. *Writing.* New York: Frederick A. Praeger, 1962.

Gleason, H. A., Jr. *An Introduction to Descriptive Linguistics.* New York: Holt, Rinehart and Winston, 1961.

Graff, Willem L. *Language and Languages.* New York: D. Appleton & Co., 1932.

Gray, Louis H. *Foundations of Language.* New York: Macmillan Co., 1939.

Greenberg, Joseph A. *Studies in African Linguistic Classification.* New Haven: Compass Publishing Co., 1955.

Guthrie, Malcolm. *The Bantu Languages of Western Equatorial Africa.* London: Oxford University Press, 1953.

————. *Languages of West Africa.* London: Oxford University Press, 1959.

————. *Non-Bantu Languages of North-Eastern Africa.* London: Oxford University Press, 1959.

————, ed. *African Language Studies I.* London: University of London, 1960.

Hockett, Charles F. *A Course in Modern Linguistics.* New York: Macmillan Co., 1958.

Hughes, John P. *The Science of Language.* New York: Random House, 1962.

India. Census Commission. *Census of India 1951.* No. 1. Languages. Delhi: Government Central Press, 1952.

Jespersen, Otto. *Language, Its Nature, Development, and Origin.* London: George Allen & Unwin 1954.

Lehmann, Winfred P. *Historical Linguistics: an Introduction.* New York: Holt, Rinehart and Winston, 1962.

Matthews, William K. *Languages of the U. S. S. R.* Cambridge, England: University Press, 1951.

Meillet, A., and M. Cohen, ed. *Les Langues du Monde.* Paris: H. Champion, 1952.

Muller, Siegfried H. *Multi-Language Recording.* (Record or tape with text manual.) Allentown, Pa.: Wible Language Institute, 1961.

North, Eric M. *The Book of a Thousand Tongues.* New York: Harper & Bros., 1938.

Paul, Albert. *Sprachenhandbuch.* Bielefeld: A. G. Ploetz, 1952.

Pei, Mario A. *The Story of Language.* Philadelphia: J. B. Lippincott Co., 1949.
_____. *Language for Everybody.* New York: Devin-Adair Co., 1956.
_____. *The World's Chief Languages.* 5th ed. New York: S. F. Vanni, 1960.
_____. *One Language for the World.* (Record with text.) New York: Folkways Records and Service Corp., 1961.
_____. *Talking Your Way around the World.* New York: Harper & Bros., 1961.
_____, and Frank Gaynor. *A Dictionary of Linguistics.* New York: Philosophical Library, 1954.

Razran, Gregory. "Transliteration of Russian," *Science,* CXXIX (1959), 1111-1113. Comments and reply in *Science,* CXXX (1959), 482-488.

Roberts, Janet. "Sociocultural Change and Communication Problems," in Frank A. Rice, ed., *Study of the Role of Second Languages in Asia, Africa, and Latin America.* Washington, D. C.: Center for Applied Linguistics of the Modern Language Association of America, 1962.

Sapir, Edward. *Language.* New York: Harcourt, Brace & Co., 1921.

Schlauch, Margaret. *The Gift of Tongues.* New York: Modern Age Books, 1942.

Steward, Julian H. *Handbook of South American Indians,* Vol. 6. Washington, D. C.: U. S. Government Printing Office, 1950.

Swanton, John R. *The Indian Tribes of North America.* Washington, D. C.: U. S. Government Printing Office, 1952.

Thieme, Paul. "The Indo-European Language," *Scientific American,* CIC, 4 (October 1958), 63-74.

Union of Soviet Socialist Republics. Tsentral'noye Statisti-cheskoye Upravleniye. *Ob Urovnye Obrazovaniya, Natsional'nom Sostavye i Vozrastnoy Strukturye Nasyelyeniya SSSR po Dannym Vsesoyuznoy Pyeryepisi Nasyelyeniya 1959 Goda.* Moscow: 1960.

United Nations. *Demographic Yearbook, 1956.* New York: United Nations, 1956.

————. *Population and Vital Statistics Report.* (Statistical Papers, Series A, Vol. XV, No. 3.) New York: United Nations, 1963.

United States. Bureau of the Census. *Sixteenth Census of the United States: 1940. Series P-15, No. 10: Population.* Washington, D. C.: U. S. Government Printing Office, 1942-43.

————. Bureau of the Census. *U. S. Census of Population 1960.* Washington, D. C.: U. S. Government Printing Office, 1962.

von Ostermann, George F. *Manual of Foreign Languages.* 4th ed. New York: Central Book Company, 1952.

Wahlgren, Erik. *The Kensington Stone, a Mystery Solved.* Madison: University of Wisconsin Press, 1958.

Walsh, Donald D. *What's What. A List of Useful Terms for the Teacher of Modern Languages.* New York: Modern Language Association of America, 1963.

Wendt, Heinz F. *Sprachen.* Frankfurt am Main: Fischer Bücherei, 1961.

The Worldmark Encyclopedia of Nations. New York: Worldmark Press, 1960.

Wycliffe Bible Translators. *Ethnologue of Bibleless Tribes.* 5th ed. and supplement. Glendale, Cal.: Wycliffe Bible Translators, 1959.

INDEX

To provide an additional function as handy reference tool, this index lists numbers of native speakers in parentheses for languages and groupings after their preferred names or spellings. *Italic type* is used for personal names, self-designations, and page numbers indicating main discussion of topic; *alt.* means "alternate name or spelling for"; *s.d.* means "self-designation for."